Landmarks of world literature

Homer

THE ODYSSEY

Landmarks of world literature

General Editor: J. P. Stern

HOMER
The Odyssey

JASPER GRIFFIN
Balliol College, Oxford

Published by the Press Syndicate of the University of Cambridge
The Pitt Building, Trumpington Street, Cambridge CB2 1RP
40 West 20th Street, New York, NY 10011-4211, USA
10 Stamford Road, Oakleigh, Victoria 3166, Australia

First published 1987
Reprinted 1989, 1992

Printed in Great Britain at
the Athenaeum Press Ltd, Newcastle upon Tyne

British Library cataloguing in publication data

Griffin, Jasper
Homer: the Odyssey.—(Landmarks of
world literature).
1. Homer, Odyssey
I. Title   II. Series
883'.01   PA4167

Library of Congress cataloguing in publication data

Griffin, Jasper
Homer, the Odyssey.
(Landmarks of world literature)
Bibliography.
1. Homer, Odyssey. 2. Odysseus (Greek mythology)
in literature.   I. Title   II. Series
PA4167.G75   1987   883'.01   87–2972

ISBN 0 521 32804 7 hardback
ISBN 0 521 31043 1 paperback

Contents

Preface

The two great epics which go under the name of Homer bring European literature into existence with a bang. Its echoes, like those of the cosmic explosion which started the universe, are still reverberating. Whatever existed of verse or prose before Homer has been lost for thousands of years, while the *Iliad* and *Odyssey* have in all that time never ceased to be read, to be admired, and to be influential. The plot of the *Odyssey* is essentially simple: the wandering hero wins his way home and faces the intruders who plan to rob him of wife, son, and kingdom. It contains unforgettable adventure stories: the Sirens, the Lotus-Eaters, the Cyclops, the Land of the Dead. It also contains comedy of manners, irony, pathos. Heroism is subjected to a quizzical scrutiny, when the hero must face ogres and witches, or conciliate a princess who finds him naked on the sea-shore, or fight a boxing match with a professional beggar. The range of characters is extraordinarily wide, and so is the breadth of interest in different social types: goddesses, queens, bards, servants, swineherds. A poem which must have emerged from a tradition of oral verse and an illiterate society, it has a sophisticated structure and an over-riding unity which is unmistakable, despite its great length and its variety of tone and subject-matter.

In this book I have aimed to put the *Odyssey* into its historical setting, and to bring out its individual character. That involves being prepared to criticise and to compare the poem with others. Every critic is, or should be, sometimes sobered, as he reflects how presumptuous it is for him to criticise great literature. Without criticism there can be little understanding; but it is at least as important for the critic to confess his own smallness in the face of a work like the *Odyssey*.

Chapter 1

The making of the *Odyssey*

1. The background to the *Odyssey*

European literature springs into existence with two great poems, the *Iliad* and the *Odyssey*, traditionally ascribed to the same poet. That, at least, is the way the Greeks thought of their own literary history, and the Romans adopted that view and transmitted it to the rest of the world. In reality, of course, such a story is impossible: works of massive scale and great sophistication do not come out of nothing, and there was a long history behind the Homeric epics. That history was dark to the Greeks, and we are obliged to use conjecture for much of it. The effort is worth making, because its results help to make many things about the poems intelligible.

The ancestors of the Greeks entered the country from the north about 1900 B.C. They belonged to the great Indo-European family of peoples, which also includes, among others, the Germanic, Celtic, Latin and Iranian peoples, and the Aryans who in the same millennium invaded and conquered Northern India. They brought with them their language and their religion. They came from a nomadic existence on the great plains; the world which they entered was one of an old and settled culture, with palaces, frescoes, writing, luxury artefacts. There was trade and correspondence between the princes of the Aegean, the Minoans as we call them, and the kingdoms of the East: Syria, Asia Minor, Egypt. The incomers came face to face with new and impressive things. They began to worship new gods and, especially, new goddesses: in addition to the old, of course, not instead of them. Their sky-god Zeus acquired a new wife, the great goddess Hera of Argos and Mycenae, and a wonderful daughter, the goddess Athena of Athens. New forms of art and music were borrowed and adapted.

Like all the Indo-European peoples, they must have brought with them heroic tales, fierce legends of warfare, cattle-raiding, adventure and revenge. The Icelandic sagas, the German Song of the Nibelungen, the English Beowulf, are among the surviving representatives of such poetry. The story of the hero who is dishonoured and avenges himself on his own companions, and the story of the hero whose wife is beset by other men while he is away on his adventures, so that he must return in time to reclaim her and take his vengeance: the basic plots of both the *Iliad* and the *Odyssey* are recognisable as being at home in that ancient tradition. But the new setting in Greece, in the midst of complex and alien societies, must have had the effect of changing and developing the old poetry, both in technique and to some extent in attitudes. We have only to think, for instance, of an *Odyssey* with no role for Athena, and showing little familiarity with ships and the sea.

Those ancestors of the Greeks set up fortresses and kingdoms, under the influence of the Minoans, at Pylos and Athens and other places; from the most spectacular of them, Mycenae in the Peloponnese, we call them Mycenaeans. They were able to amass treasures of gold and ivory, to trade with the East, and to have bureaucracies of surprising extent and complexity, whose clerkly records, the 'Linear B tablets', let us see something of the workings of centralised kingdoms where everything was listed and inventoried: the lists of chariot wheels, for instance, faithfully record the presence of broken ones. All this was swept away, and the art of writing was lost, in the disasters of the twelfth century B.C., in which the citadels, including that of Mycenae, were destroyed. A dark age followed, with reduced population, humble conditions of life (no more stone palaces), and sharp decline both in the arts and in overseas connections. The cause of this catastrophe is generally identified as the coming of the Dorians, another group of Greeks who were slower than the rest to enter Greece, having stayed behind somewhere up in the north west. Intercourse with the East resumed on an appreciable scale by about 850 B.C., and the next two centuries

⌐v a great increase in oriental products, rituals, and tech-
⌐ques such as building and jewellery. It was at this time that
⌐he Greeks took from Phoenicia the alphabet, dramatically
improving it by the device of writing out the vowels as
separate letters, and so creating the ancestor of our own
alphabet. This new literacy of Greece was quite unconnected
with the old, and the epic poets imagined their heroes as illiterate in a world without writing.

What is the relevance of all this to Homer? The Greeks
knew nothing about the man, or the name, to which they
ascribed the greatest treasures of their literature. They could
not even agree where he had lived: in the words of the
epigram,

> Seven rich cities contend for Homer dead,
> Through which the living Homer begged his bread.

The name 'Homeros' is an unusual though not unique one,
and it may seem reasonable to suppose that the reason why
it became attached to the great epics was because there was
indeed a brilliant singer who was called by it. In the absence,
however, of any reliable biographical data, we fall back with
particular urgency on what can be known about the
antecedents of these extraordinary poems.

It emerges, then, that three strands of influence can be
detected, although they cannot always be separated: the Indo-
European inheritance of stories of heroism; the impact of the
sophisticated world of the Aegean in the second millennium
B.C.; and the atmosphere of the time of the actual creation
of the poems, about 700 B.C. The last of the three was
doubtless the most important. It was the time when Greece
was first taking on what we think of as her classical form. In
metal work, sculpture, architecture, pottery, the influence of
Oriental and Egyptian motifs and skills led to the creation of
imposing works on the grand scale. New Greek cities — 'colonies' — were being founded, all the way from Marseille to
Cyrene, and from Sicily to the Black Sea. The influence of
Oriental literature is more controversial, but the discoveries
of the twentieth century strongly suggest that along with the

alphabet the Greeks owed something to the poetry of
East. Yet, in the words of the *Epinomis*, a dialogue attribut•
to Plato but probably written by one of his pupils, 'Whateve.
Greeks take over from foreigners, they make it better in the
end.'

Thus Oriental parallels can be found, especially in the
literature of Phoenician Ugarit, but also in Sumerian,
Babylonian, and Assyrian poetry, for the basic form of the
Homeric poems, narrative in a long verse repeated (like blank
verse in English) *ad infinitum*, without any kind of stanza or
refrain; for the fixed epithets ('the broad earth', and 'the
father of gods and men' actually are fixed expressions in
Oriental poems); for the typical scenes and the council
meetings of gods; for the mountain of the gods which is 'in
the North', like the Greek Olympus; for the exact repetition,
when a speech is reported to a third party, of the whole of the
speech. The very ancient Epic of Gilgamesh has parallels even
for such things as the profound and pessimistic meditation of
the *Iliad* on the inevitable doom of man and the tragic nature
of heroism, and for the techniques, so striking in the *Odyssey*,
of starting the poem with two main characters in separate
places, who are then brought together, and of including in the
poem a character who narrates events from an earlier past
(Utnapishtim, the counterpart of Noah, who tells Gilgamesh
the story of the Flood).

No one, we know, ever said anything for the first time. The
poet of the *Odyssey* would certainly not have claimed to be
the first poet in the history of the world. This brief historical
sketch may serve to give some idea of the complex situation into
which he came: a time when Greece was emerging from a dark
age into a new and exciting period of progress, expanding
horizons, adventures in all the art forms. Behind the dark
period lay unforgotten memories of the great king in Mycenae
rich in gold, and an age of great achievements and splendid
heroism, magnified by nostalgia and glorified by song and
story through the bleak centuries that had intervened. And
above all, perhaps, a singer of genius had recently produced a
great and original poem, the *Iliad* (see section 13 below).

2. The date of the *Odyssey*

The almost unanimous view of the Greeks was that *Iliad* and *Odyssey* were composed by the same man, the blind singer Homer. Only a few heretics, known as 'separators', *chōrizontes*, ascribed them to different poets. His date was as uncertain as his place, and we fall back on internal arguments from the poems themselves. They contain elements of high antiquity: the memory of Mycenae as 'rich in gold', for instance, which it had not been since about 1150 B.C., and of the great king Minos of Crete. They also contain archaic verbal forms and phrases, and a sprinkling of words whose meaning was evidently obscure to singers and audience alike, but which were felt to belong to the dignity of heroic epic.

The reader who is surprised by this might try the experiment of reading a couple of pages of *Hamlet*, which sounds intelligible enough in the theatre, and seeing how many expressions they contain whose meaning, if it is to be made clear, requires recourse to explanatory notes or to a dictionary. Such words are *dasplētis*, used once of the avenging Fury (*Odyssey* 15.234) and conventionally translated 'fierce', or *audēessa*, 'speaking', used of goddesses in the strange phrase *deinē theos audēessa*, 'dread goddess with speech' (*Odyssey* 10.150 etc.). This is strikingly paralleled in the Gilgamesh epic, where the queen of the gods is called 'good at the shout'; perhaps a phrase already mysterious in the Oriental epic had entered the Greek tradition and remained there, hallowed if opaque?

In addition, the poems are consciously set in a past which was different from the singer's own time. In those days, for instance, men fought and chopped wood with bronze, not iron, and in both epics that practice is kept up pretty consistently. But at moments the reality of the Iron Age shows through. It is revealing that the most conspicuous slip is in the phrase, twice repeated, 'iron of itself draws men on to fight' (16.294, 19.13): that is evidently a proverb, and its familiarity has enabled it to slip under the poet's guard. Again, the epics are set in a world before the coming of the Dorians. Places which in the post-Mycenaean period were inhabited by Dorians, such as Argos and Sparta, are in the poems the home of Achaeans, and Dorians are unheard of. But very occasionally there is a slip. Listing the peoples who live on Crete, Odysseus sticks too close to the historic truth and includes 'Dorians who are *trichāikes*' (19.177) − another mysterious adjective, perhaps referring to their hair-style: while the *Iliad*, too, which never mentions Dorians, does once, in a digression, refer to a place called Dorion (*Iliad* 2.594), a name which presupposes Dorian inhabitants, as Sussex presupposes Saxons.

A few physical objects occur in the poems which seem to belong definitely to the second millennium B.C., such as the 'silver-studded sword', a regular phrase (e.g. *Odyssey* 8.406), which seems to have been in the poetic tradition ever since such swords were in regular use, in the fifteenth century B.C. Other examples are such things as Helen's silver work-basket on wheels (*Odyssey* 4.131), and the unique helmet adorned with boar's tusks which is described − and described as if it were an heirloom − at *Iliad* 10.261. But it can be said that in general, despite the presence both of genuinely ancient elements and also of deliberate stylisation, the world assumed in the epics is that of the eighth century or so B.C. That will emerge in section 18. What must have taken time to evolve is the artificial dialect − 'Homeric Greek' − in which the epics are composed. It was never spoken, and while it presents a coherent appearance it contains elements from different dialects, mixed with some which were created within the epic tradition and never existed outside it. Moreover, two other types of evidence point in the same direction. One is the mention of such things as temples for the gods (e.g. *Odyssey* 6.9 and 12.346), in place of the old outdoor worship: temples begin to appear in Greece about 800 B.C. About 750 a new style of warfare came in, the solid phalanx of uniformly armed men ('hoplites') which was to be characteristic of classical Greece. The Homeric poems, which in general portray war as an affair of duels between individual aristocrats, show in a number of places familiarity with this sort of

.ighting and the new style of armour it required. The latest instances of such definitely datable items come from about 725
or 700 B.C., and it is striking that it is almost at the same time
— 700 to 675 — that scenes from the epics begin to be fre-
quent in vase painting. By 650 or so the poems were clearly
in existence, and probably, as we shall see in section 13, the
Odyssey was slightly later than the *Iliad* and strongly influenced by it. We shall not go far wrong if we think that the
Iliad was composed not later than 700, and the *Odyssey* not
later than 675 B.C. Fortunately, in the words of G. S. Kirk,
'In the light of our ignorance of so much that went on in the
ninth and eighth centuries, and even in the first half of the
seventh, it must be confessed that our inability to place the
poems more precisely does not at present matter very much.'

3. Bards and oral poetry

Homer was imagined by later Greeks as a blind singer, travel-
ling about and making a living by his songs. In the *Odyssey*
we find a blind singer, Demodocus; the poet tells us that
'The Muse loved him exceedingly, and she gave him both
good and evil: she robbed him of his eyes, but she gave him
sweet song' (8.63–4). That objective but pregnant account
reminds us of other Homeric figures: the blind prophet
Tiresias, whom Odysseus must consult in the world of the
dead (10.493, 12.267), and the virtuous Amphiaraus,
descended from a family of hereditary prophets: 'Zeus of the
aegis and Apollo loved him exceedingly with all kinds of love,
and he did not come to the threshold of old age' (15.245–6).
In the *Iliad* there is another singer, Thamyris, who was so
proud of his skill that he challenged the Muses themselves:
'and in their anger they maimed him and took away his lovely
song and made him forget his music' (*Iliad* 2.599–600).

At one level there is an explanation of this pattern in the
fact that in early society a blind man may make a living as a
singer or as the possessor of hidden knowledge, a second sight
which flourishes in the absence of the first; but also there
seems to be implied the likelihood of an intimate connection

between such gifts and special suffering. He whom the god love dies young, according to a later Greek proverb, and unusual gifts, while they are a sign of divine favour, mark their owner out for grief. And while it is the function of song to give delight, *terpein* (1.347, 8.429), yet epic song can arise only out of suffering and sorrow.

Not all singers are blind, however: Phemius, who sings to the suitors while Odysseus is away, can see perfectly well. Singers, in the *Odyssey*, are in principle wanderers. 'Nobody invites beggars', says the good swineherd Eumaeus to the haughty suitor Antinous:

Who does invite a stranger from elsewhere, except indeed for one of those who are skilled men, a prophet or a healer of the sick or a worker in wood, or an inspired singer who gives delight with his song? They are the men who are invited, all over the world.

(*Odyssey* 17.382–6)

Phemius, pleading for his life when the suitors are slain, says

It was not by my will that I would come into your house to sing to the Suitors at their feasts: they were more numerous and stronger, and they would bring me here by force.   (22.351–3)

Even among the Phaeacians, rich and luxurious, the singer Demodocus is apparently not one of the king's household but summoned from outside when he is wanted (8.43–5, 62). The *Odyssey* is interested in these professional singers, who are treated with respect. Phemius' prayer for his life is immediately granted, and Demodocus is actually sent, by Odysseus, the most highly regarded cut of meat, with the words

There, give this meat to Demodocus to eat, and I greet him, for all my sorrows: among all men on earth singers receive honour and respect, for the Muse has taught them their songs, and she loves the race of singers.   (8.477–81)

Perhaps a certain hint of propaganda is discernible on behalf of the poet's own kind.

That the poet was a singer and not a writer is a fact of greater importance than was generally recognised before the twentieth century, in which the evidence already present in the

text of Homer has been combined with detailed study of the
ways of illiterate bards in other countries, to form an important theory about the nature of the poems. It is an obvious
fact about the *Iliad* and *Odyssey* that they behave differently
from most other poetry in the matter of repetitions. Speeches
begin with formal addresses and indications of utterance,
some of which recur constantly. Thus when Odysseus meets
the shade of Achilles among the dead,

With a groan he uttered winged words: 'Zeus-born son of Laertes,
Odysseus of many plans . . .' So he spoke, and I addressed him in
answer; 'O Achilles, son of Peleus, greatest by far of the Achaeans
. . .'   (11.471ff)

Here we have four lines, each of which recurs again and
again. 'With a groan he uttered winged words' comes seven
times in the *Odyssey* and three times in the *Iliad*, the line addressing Odysseus by his name and titles comes fifteen times
in the *Odyssey*, and seven times in the *Iliad*, the next line fifteen times in the *Odyssey*, and the address to Achilles twice
in the *Iliad*.

These lines marking the beginning and end of speeches are
in fact rather a special case: the incidence of exactly repeated
phrases in them is higher than in any other category of
Homeric verse. Their function must have been to slow the
pace of events and to mark a pause between one utterance and
another. What the characters say is often emotional and
usually contributes something new and interesting to the progress of events; these stately lines, recalling the heroic rank of
the speakers and marking off their speeches, resemble the few
stereotyped notes on the continuo between arias in an opera
by Mozart. But every reader of Homer is struck by the regular
return of fixed epithets − swift ship, unploughed sea, long-
haired Achaeans, grey-eyed goddess Athena. It has traditionally presented difficulties that such epithets recur imper-
turbably in places where they seem more or less incongruous.
That Achilles is 'swift-footed Achilles' even when sitting
down, or a ship 'a swift ship' even when motionless, is less
disturbing. We can talk of 'a fast car' even when it is not in

motion, and that looks like a parallel: in reality it is not, as
the English phrase distinguishes one sort of car from another,
while an Odyssean line like 12.292 'Let us prepare our meal
beside our swift ship' has no such implication, but means if
pressed (as it is not intended to be pressed) something like
'beside our ship – which naturally possesses the qualities appropriate to a ship in a heroic epic'.

The next stage of oddity is the reappearance of epithets
from narrative into speech. Thus the poet describes Odysseus
and Telemachus moving swiftly into action to remove the
weapons from the walls of the hall: 'They then darted forward, Odysseus and his brilliant son' (19.21). It comes as a
surprise, though, when in the middle of the fight for their
lives the disloyal servant Melanthius, offering to go and fetch
weapons for the Suitors, says 'That is where they put them,
Odysseus and his brilliant son' (22.141). That is not the way
people talk about their enemies. Nor is it life-like, when
Odysseus tells his supporters, after the slaughter of the
Suitors, 'Then clean the splendid chairs and the tables with
water and with sponges with many holes' (22.438–9). That
evidently comes from the narrative use, a few lines later:
'Then they cleaned the splendid chairs and the tables with
water and with sponges with many holes' (22.452–3). The
epithets, stately and only a little quaint in narrative, become
bizarre in the giving of an order. As with Odysseus' brilliant
son, and with the swift ship, the adjectives are not meant to
be pressed.

Something similar must be said of Penelope taking a cup-
board key 'in her sturdy hand' (21.6), an epithet evidently
meant less for ladies than for heroes taking up spears in battle; we should not invent subtle justifications for such
passages, as people still do. The 'shining clothes' which
Nausicaa takes to wash (6.74) are no different: clothes nor-
mally are clean and shining in the heroic world, and the fact
that these are dirty is not fully felt. When the swineherd
Eumaeus says that if Odysseus had only come home he would
have given to his loyal retainer 'a house and a plot of land and
a much courted wife' (14.64), the epithet 'much courted'

..ggests a daughter of a noble house, not at all the sort of girl
.or a swineherd, however trusty; and in fact it is elsewhere
used only of Penelope, beset by her hundred suitors (4.770,
23.249). Again it would doubtless be inept to build on this
epithet a psychological account of Eumaeus' pathetic hopes
for social climbing. Sometimes epithets are used rather loose-
ly, but in general they are appropriate and exact − the swift
black ships, the tall trees, the clattering horses − and their
constant recurrence, keeping all things before our mind's eye
in their sharply seen essence, contributes a great deal to the
style, clear yet noble, of Homeric verse.

The oral poet faces particular problems. He must keep his
song going, and that involves fitting the constantly unfolding
pattern of events to an elaborate and exacting metre. The
Homeric hexameter is a long line consisting of patterns of
'long' and 'short' syllables (there is no stress accent in early
Greek). The basic unit of the line is the dactyl, $-\cup\cup$ ($-$ =
long syllable, $\cup$ = short syllable). The two short (or 'light')
syllables might be replaced by one long (or 'heavy') syllable.
The line, as its name 'hexameter' suggests, consists of six of
these dactyls, except that the last in the line marks the end of
a rhythmical unit by a slight variation: not $-\cup\cup$ but $-\cup$. The
line thus consisted of a minimum number of twelve syllables,
which is very rare, in fact: for instance

> tō d' en Messēnēi xumblētēn allēloiin.   (21.157)
> (the pair met in Messene).

The maximum is seventeen, which is common: for instance

> ton d' apameibomenos prosephē polymētis Odysseus.
>   (7.207 and repeatedly)
> (to him in answer spoke Odysseus of many plans).

The singer accompanied himself on the *phorminx*, or lyre:
probably more to support the rhythm than to produce start-
ling musical effects. The Homeric line is quite unusually
long, complex, and exacting for oral epic, especially as there
are other conventions governing such things as the points in
the line where word division takes place. Some points are
avoided for this, others cultivated; and there is a strong

tendency for the line to divide into two slightly uneven halves, the second half being a little longer than the first, and also into four quarters, not equal in length. Some typical lines:

> andra moi / ennepe, Mousa, / polutropon, / hos mala polla
> (Sing me, Muse, the man of many travels)   (1.1)
>
> pollōn d' / anthrōpōn / iden astea / kai noon egnō   (1.3)
> (He saw the cities of many peoples and knew their minds)
>
> autōn gar / spheterēsin / atasthaliēsin / olonto   (1.7)
> (For they perished through their own sin)
>
> kourē / Īkarioio, / periphrōn / Pēnelopeia   (1.329)
> (The daughter of Icarius, the prudent Penelope).

The singer must fit his material to this elaborate frame, in addition to remaining within the artificial dialect and the elevated style and special vocabulary associated with epic song. Not only this: he must be prepared for interventions and pressures from his audience. The ideal he aims at, indeed, is to have them under his spell. That is the effect which Odysseus himself produces on the Phaeacians, when he tells them his tales: King Alcinous says to him 'We do not take you for a deceiver and a cheat, one of the many liars whom the black earth supports; your utterance is shapely, and your mind discreet. You have told your tale like a singer . . .' (11.363ff): like Homer himself, in fact. The result on the Phaeacian audience was, as the poet twice tells us, that 'He finished speaking, and they were all profoundly silent, held by enchantment in the shadowy hall' (11.33–4; 13.1–2). That 'enchantment', by the way, is to be understood in something like a literal sense. We are to imagine an audience of strong and unselfconscious reactions, not jaded by constant watching of television; and the power of the word over them was great. In countries like Greece and Italy it is still stronger today than in northern Europe; and several centuries after Homer's time the philosopher Plato objected to the watching of tragedy, because it had too engrossing an emotional impact on the audience.

That was the aim of the singer, but it is clear from the

Odyssey that the enchantment was not always achieved. Phemius, singing to the Suitors of the return of the Achaeans from Troy, is dominating his audience — 'The famous bard was singing to them, and they were sitting and listening in silence' (1.325) — when Penelope suddenly appears and interrupts, asking for a different theme instead of this harrowing one, the tale of events which have robbed her of her husband (1.337ff). Demodocus, too, the singer of Phaeacia, is repeatedly interrupted when his songs of the Trojan War make Odysseus weep.

Alcinous, who sat next to Odysseus, heard his heavy sobs, and at once he spoke out among the Phaeacian lords of the oar: 'Listen, you leaders and rulers of the Phaeacians: now we have had our fill both of dinner and of the lyre which is the partner of the feast . . .'
(8.95–9)

Again later Alcinous stops Demodocus:

Listen, you leaders and rulers of the Phaeacians: let Demodocus now check his tuneful lyre, for what he is singing is not to the liking of everyone . . .   (8.537–8)

The singer must be aware of the response of his audience, and there can be no doubt that on different occasions he would sing different versions of any song — longer or shorter, more or less decorated, emphasising one feature or another, even taking different versions of the same story. We shall return to this important question in sections 6 and 10.

The consequence of all this was that the singer did not simply repeat his songs by rote. On the other hand, he also did not improvise them on the spot out of wholly unpremeditated material. He had in his mind a range of recurrent and typical scenes: the launching of a ship, the preparing and consuming of a feast, the arrival of an unexpected person, a duel between heroes, the despatch and mission of a messenger, and so on. These scenes could be extended or compressed, combined or varied. He also had at his disposal an extensive and supple range of formulaic phrases and expressions, ways of referring to individual heroes and gods, phrases for simple acts such as 'drew his sword' or 'smote the water with their oars' or 'dawn broke'. It is the existence and the range of these systems which explains much which can seem unfamiliar about the poetry of Homer; and they derive their function from the oral nature of the Greek epic tradition.

4. The language of the *Odyssey* and the 'formulaic system'

It is easy to give examples of formulae which form a regular system. The hero Odysseus is of course mentioned many times in the *Odyssey*, and it was an obvious convenience to have ready-made ways of referring to him which fitted the hexameter line and complied with the stylistic level of the epic. The metrical form of his name, $\upsilon - -$, fits well in to the final position in the line, and we find the poet constantly putting it there. He extends it to the convenient length $- \upsilon\upsilon - -$ by putting before it the elevated but colourless epithet *dīos*, 'noble': *dīos Odusseus* comes at the end of more than seventy lines of the Odyssey, often preceded by a verb (*hupoleípeto*, 'was left behind', for instance, or *enērato*, 'slew'). That enables the poet to produce an elegant half line. But he may want to extend the name of his hero a little further: $\upsilon\upsilon - \upsilon\upsilon - -$. In that case he becomes *polymētis Odusseus*, 'Odysseus of many plans'. That makes it possible to put a rather shorter verb, for instance, before the name of the hero, especially a verb for 'spoke', *prosephē*: more than seventy lines have as their second half *prosephē polumētis Odusseus*, 'spoke Odysseus of many plans'. But in the rarer case (three instances) where a naturally short vowel stood at the end of the word which was to precede $\upsilon\upsilon - \upsilon$ *Odusseus*, the rules of Homeric metre required a more massive group of consonants than the *p* of *polymétis*, in order to produce the effect of 'lengthening' the awkward short vowel. In that case Odysseus ceased to be 'of many plans' and became 'city-sacker', *ptoliporthos Odusseus*: so, for instance, at 8.3 *ōrto ptoliporthos Odusseus*, 'Odysseus city-sacker arose'. It was also often convenient to take up the whole of the second half of the verse with the hero's name, not just the last quarter: in that

:ase he becomes — thirty-two times — *polutlās dīos Odusseus*, 'much-enduring noble Odysseus', u − − −uu − −.

Now, Odysseus was, of course, noble, and a planner, and long suffering, and city-sacker (the title no doubt relates to his devising of the wooden horse which led to the capture of Troy); the system is concerned to be appropriate, and it never (for instance) gives wily Odysseus the regular epithet of the dashing Achilles, *podas ōkus*, 'swift of foot', although *podas ōkus Odusseus* would scan just as well as *polumētis Odusseus*. But clearly it would be inappropriate to find reasons other than metrical convenience for the choice of one of these qualities of Odysseus rather than another, in a particular passage of the poem. Similar patterns can be found for other prominent persons, such as Penelope and Telemachus. This point is an important one, but it is also important not to exaggerate it.

First, despite the formal elegance and wide extension of such systems of formulae involving proper names, it remains true that the name of Odysseus occurs more often in the *Odyssey* with no epithet at all than with one. Similarly, while there are recurrent phrases with epithets for the sea, they are used only in one in three of the allusions to the sea in the poem. Second, it must be remembered that ancient Greek is a highly inflected language, like Latin: modern German gives some idea of grammatical inflection, but has only a remnant by the standards of the ancient languages. That means that the name of Odysseus, like any other noun, will appear in different forms in accordance with its grammatical function in the sentence. *Odusseus* is the form of his name only if he is the subject of the verb; if he is the object, if someone or something looks at him or insults him or misses him, then his name has the form *Odussĕă*, and all the subject formulae are unusable. If he is the possessor of something, or has something given to him, then two more forms (*Odussēŏs, Odussēī*) must be accommodated in the verse. For these cases there are no systems comparable, in elegance and economy, with that for Odysseus as subject, and a much wider range of solutions is found. We are not to suppose that there existed sets of formulae which would generate poems more or less automatically.

It will be helpful to give an example on a more extended scale of the way in which the poet can use his stock of lines and motifs. What follows is a fairly unstressed passage, the summoning by Telemachus of a public meeting (*agorē*) of the people of Ithaca, the first for twenty years, in his attempt to mobilise public opinion against the Suitors. The meeting itself will be very lively, with a full range of contrasting speeches and Telemachus reduced to bursting into tears, but the introduction is dispassionate:

> ēmos d' ērigeneia phanē rhododaktulos ēōs,
> ornut' ar' ex eunēphin Odussēos philos hūios,
> heimata hessamenos, peri de xiphos oxu thet' ōmōi,
> possi d' hupo liparoisin edēsato kāla pedīla,
> 5 bē d' imen ek thalamoio theōi enalinkios antēn.
> aipsa de kērūkessi liguphthongoisi keleuse
> kērussein agorēnde karē komoōntas Achaious.
> hoi men ekērusson, toi d' ēgeironto mal' ōka.
> autar epei r' ēgerthen homēgerees t' egenonto,
> 10 bē r' imen eis agorēn, palamēi d' eche chalkeon enchos
> ouk oios, hama tōi ge duō kunes argoi heponto.
>
> (*Odyssey* 2.1–11)

(When early-rising rose-fingered Dawn appeared, / then the dear son of Odysseus rose from his bed, / putting on his clothes, and about his shoulder he slung his sword, / and under his smooth feet he fastened his fine sandals, / and he left his bedroom like a god to meet. / At once he instructed the clear-voiced summoners / to summon the long-haired Achaeans to a meeting. / They cried their summons, and the people were soon assembled. / Then when they had assembled and come together, / he made his entrance into the meeting-place, and in his hand he held a bronze spear. / He was not unaccompanied: two nimble dogs followed him.) [In the translation I have indicated with an oblique line the end of each verse of the Greek.]

That is a representative example of a routine piece of Homeric narration. It opens with a beautiful and memorable line comparing the rays of dawn to the extended fingers of a hand, the colour of a rose; it goes on to a competent account of Telemachus' preparations, and it then presents him making his first public appearance. Athena, the poet goes on to say, shed grace on him, and the people gazed in admiration as he took his father's seat (a moment pregnant with symbolism: the young prince starts to assert himself as king — but without success). We see him, an outdoor young man, with his dogs at his heels. In the passage there is not a single phrase which does not occur elsewhere in identical form, and whole groups of lines also are found elsewhere. The first line appears altogether twenty times in the *Odyssey* and twice in the *Iliad*. It is a perfect line, and the singer felt no need to try to improve on it. Of the second line, the first half is used twice elsewhere in the *Odyssey* (of Nestor getting out of bed, 3.405; of Menelaus, 4.307), and the second half, a periphrasis for Telemachus, recurs four times. The next three lines occur unchanged at 4.308–10, the rising of Menelaus; only the first two (lines 3 and 4 here) at 20.125–6, again of Telemachus; while line 4 also appears four times in the *Iliad*. Line 5, as we have seen, appears in the same context in the fourth book of the *Odyssey*; it is also notable that the first half appears again in the *Iliad*, where it is used of the goddess Hera leaving her toilette to seduce her husband Zeus, *Iliad* 14.188 ('he' and 'she' are not expressed in the Greek), while the second half closely resembles the phrase used in the *Iliad* of the summoner Talthybius, *theōi enalinkios audēn*, 'like a god in voice'.

The next lines, which describe the summoning of an assembly, recur in the *Iliad*, which contains more assemblies, but not in the *Odyssey*: with a variant for the first three words of line 6, lines 6–8 recur identically at *Iliad* 2.50–2; later in the same book of the *Iliad*, when the assembly is over and the men move off to fight, they recur again (*Iliad* 2.442–4), but this time with the substitution for *agorēnde* ('to a meeting') of the word *polemonde* ('to war'). This illustrates the suppleness of these formulae: as with the possibility of completing 'like a god . . .' in two different ways which both fit perfectly, so the change of one word for another which is metrically equivalent enables the singer to use a group of three lines in two different contexts. The tenth line is a little less straightforward, as the poems are not usually concerned to represent the *first* appearance of a hero at an assembly. such gatherings were a routine part of the hero's life, his ambition to be 'a speaker of words and a doer of deeds' (*Iliad* 9.443). Line 10 is composed of elements which all do recur. 'He made his entrance into the meeting-place' comes at *Odyssey* 20.146 (a weak passage, where Telemachus is simply got out of the house for a little for the poet's own purposes and there is no meeting); 'and in his hand he held a bronze spear' is used of Athena when she arrives at Odysseus' house in disguise, 1.104, while the phrase 'a bronze spear' at the end of the line is a very common one, appearing seventeen times in the *Iliad* and five times in the *Odyssey*. Thus we see that the common 'a bronze spear', useful primarily for descriptions of fighting, is extended, in the rarer peacetime context, with 'and in his hand he held'; that produces half a line which fits smoothly with another half line.

Finally, line 11, the two dogs. 'Two nimble dogs followed him' is a phrase which occurs three times in the *Odyssey*, but the line as a whole is more interesting than that simple fact. It is a regular feature of the Homeric world that a lady does not appear alone in company, especially the company of men. When Penelope comes among the Suitors, she comes

> ouk oiē, hama tēi ge kai amphipoloi du' heponto
> > (*Odyssey* 1.331, etc.)
> (Not unaccompanied, with her followed two maids)

Three times that line is used of Penelope in the *Odyssey*, and once of a very different lady, the guilty and remorseful Helen of the *Iliad* (*Iliad* 3.143). There is a family resemblance between that line and the one which describes Telemachus accompanied by two dogs, as we see when we add some other members of the family:

> Not unaccompanied, with him two menservants followed
> > (*Iliad* 24.573)
> Not unaccompanied, with him went Helen and Megapenthes
> > (*Odyssey* 15.100)

(of Menelaus with his wife and his son).

> Not unaccompanied, with him went the two sons of Antenor
> > (*Iliad* 2.822)

.t is not only that 'not unaccompanied, with him/her . . .' provides a convenient half line, which can be completed with maids or manservants or dogs or other heroes; the number two seems to come naturally in such lines. We may even find a hint of it in a verse like *Odyssey* 10.208, when Eurylochus reluctantly leads his scouting party on Circe's island:

Off he went, with him two and twenty companions . . .

Why that number? Because the shape of the verse suggested the number two. Some of the older commentators enmeshed themselves in problems on the question how many men Odysseus had at this time and how he reached that number: we can see that such questions are not the point.

The point is that the exigencies of performing in the epic tradition led to a kind of poetry in which the unit of composition tended not to be the word, as it is in most of the verse familiar to us, but the phrase: sometimes a substantial sentence or more, occupying several lines of the poem. Everywhere in the *Iliad* and the *Odyssey* the attachment of nouns and epithets tends to grow fixed and regular; a particular verb tends to occur regularly at the same point of the line; phrases are repeated, or others are modelled on the sound of them. In the case of *theōi enalinkios antēn* and *theōi enalinkios audēn*, 'like a god to meet' and 'like a god in voice', the close resemblance of sound has clearly played the decisive part.

At another level, we see in the *Odyssey* the importance of the typical scene. The poet has in his repertoire a large number of patterns for scenes, which it is a great part of his skill to vary and arrange. In the *Odyssey* there are, for instance, a great many scenes concerning the arrival of a stranger and the offer to him of hospitality. There is a definite series of events which should follow. The stranger should be greeted, welcomed, invited in, and offered a meal. After he has eaten, he can with good manners be asked who he is and where he comes from (that is made explicit at *Odyssey* 3.69–70 and 4.60–1). The guest may be given a bath and bedded down for the night; at parting the host should give

him a present (*xeinion*). This outline can be filled in wit.
details. The question of the identity of the guest, for instance,
can be made into a little drama. Helen, who shows herself
cleverer than her husband at every turn, is quick to guess the
identity of Telemachus (4.137ff). With Odysseus among the
Phaeacians the moment of self-revelation is delayed enormously: he is asked after his first meal 'Who are you?'
(7.238), but he contrives to conceal his identity for another
seven hundred lines, giving hints by his behaviour at dinner
the next evening (8.83, 522) but finally answering only at 9.19
– 'I am Odysseus son of Laertes, famous among all men for
my cunning, and my reputation has reached to the sky . . .'

The meal can be a sacrificial feast to a god, as with the
people of Pylos in Book Three, or a wedding, as with Menelaus
in Book Four, and that allows for developments and variations. At dinner the company may tell of their experiences
(Nestor, 3.103ff; Menelaus, 4.343; Odysseus, 9.19–12.453),
or a singer may tell a story (8.266ff). The motif of presents
also lends itself to various developments. Villains, as we shall
see, offer monstrous parodies of the gifts which are the due
of a guest. The moment of presentation can be disposed of in
half a line ('There they spent the night, and he gave them
presents': 15.187), or it can be developed into one or more
separate scenes, as when Odysseus is given not only presents
by his host, King Alcinous, but also a special gift by a tactless
Phaeacian who has insulted him, and in addition gifts by
Queen Arete which he packs in a box and fastens with a
special knot which Circe taught him (8.401–48). From the
Phaeacians Odysseus receives fabulously lavish gifts, 'bronze
and gold in plenty and garments, so rich that Odysseus would
not have brought so much from Troy if he had come
unscathed, bringing his share of the booty' (5.39–41;
13.135–7). That enables the poet to remedy his hero's losses,
a point to which he, like Odysseus, attaches great importance
(see section 19). Again, the motif can be made into a little
comedy of manners. Menelaus, well meaning but obtuse,
offers Telemachus a gift of horses and chariot: Telemachus
must tactfully decline, explaining that Ithaca is too rocky for

horses (4.589–619). Good-natured Menelaus offers a silver
gilt bowl instead; but as he makes the gift he is upstaged –
as usual – by his wife Helen, who appears with a gift of her
own, a dress for Telemachus' wife when he gets married, 'a
keepsake of the hands of Helen' (15.112–30). She knows the
extra value which that provenance will give it.

Conversely, there may be breaches of hospitality. When the
disguised Athena arrives in Ithaca to speak to Telemachus,
the Suitors take no notice of her coming (1.103–22); they go
on with their games and their noise, and Telemachus and his
guest are forced to whisper (1.156–7). No wonder Athena
comments unfavourably on their manners:

Tell me the truth now: what is this feasting, what is this throng?
What is its function? Is it a celebration or a wedding? Evidently it
is not a dinner by subscription. They looked to me like violent and
arrogant men dining in this house. Any decent newcomer would be
shocked by the sight of all their outrages.   (1.224–9)

This establishes the theme for the terrible wrongness of
Odysseus' eventual arrival home. He is insulted by the servants (17.215ff, 18.321ff, 19.6ff) and mocked and abused by
the Suitors, who throw things at him in his own house;
Ctesippus, one of the Suitors, actually says 'I will give this
man a present (*xeinion*)' – and throws a cow's hoof at him
(20.296). That recalls the monstrous behaviour of the
Cyclops, who promises a present to Odysseus in return for his
good wine and then says 'I will devour you last, after your
companions, the others first: that shall be your present'
(9.369–70). The Cyclops is duly punished for this grisly offence against hospitality, and when Ctesippus is slain the virtuous oxherd exults over his corpse: 'That is a present for you
in return for the hoof you bestowed on the god-like Odysseus'
(22.290). These scenes of the perversion of hospitality are to
be appreciated in the light of the repeated examples of true
hospitality, and collectively they all contribute a central
strand to the moral pattern of the poem: both Odysseus and
Penelope say of the slaughter of the Suitors, using identical
words, 'It is the gods who have killed them, for they respected
nobody in the world, high or low, who came among them'

(22.413–16, 23.63–6). At the opposite extreme of insignificance we can see how the poet can reduce the theme to a minimum – he does not like to omit it:

The sun went down and all ways were darkened, and they arrived at Pherae, at the house of Diocles, the son of Ortilochus son of Alpheius. There they spent the night, and he gave them presents. And when early rising rose-fingered dawn appeared, they yoked their horses and mounted the bright chariot and drove away.

(15.185–91)

It is not possible to discuss at length many such themes and the scenes which they can generate. They include such things as the preparing and eating of a meal, the sending and arrival of a messenger, the soliloquy and decision of a character facing a difficult choice, the appearance of a lady among a lively company of men, the description of a storm and shipwreck. In all these cases we find both the exact repetition of lines and of the order of events, and also rich variety. The preparing and eating of a meal is a mark of civilisation and good-fellowship: there are monstrous perversions of it when the Cyclops devours Odysseus' men – 'Cutting them limb from limb he prepared his meal' (9.291), or the Laestrygonians, 'spearing them like fishes they made their loathsome feast' (10.124), or King Agamemnon and his men are slaughtered at table:

You have been present at many a killing, when men have been killed singly or in pitched battle, but that sight would have made you grieve more than any other, as we lay by the wine bowl and the tables heaped with food, while the floor ran with blood. (11.416–20)

That looks forward to the slaughter of the Suitors at their feast in Book Twenty-Two, where Antinous is shot through the throat as he sits drinking, and his feet kick over the table, while the food is splashed with blood (22.15–20).

The motif of the corrupted feast, we see, is not only varied but also developed in a crescendo as the poem proceeds. That is an argument for the coherent conception and structure of the poem. Something similar can be seen in the relationship between the landing of Odysseus on the coast of the Phaeacians, where he makes his way with the help of Nausicaa and Athena to the king's palace, and his arrival on the coast of Ithaca, where he makes his way with the help of Eumaeus and Athena to his own palace. The second series of incidents is clearly akin to the first, but it is even longer and fuller in development, appropriately to its position in the story and the poem. Penelope appears among the Suitors in Book One, where she is soon packed off by her son; she appears again, with identical lines of introduction in Book Eighteen (1.331–5; 18.207–11), and there the scene is much longer, more varied, and more emotional. Again, a climax to the theme. The oral technique did allow the poet to give his long poem a coherent and memorable structure.

5. Is the *Odyssey* an oral poem?

Up to now we have been talking as if the *Odyssey* were certainly oral, the creation of a singer or singers more or less like the Demodocus and the Phemius whom we find performing within it. Strictly speaking that cannot be proved. The poem reaches us in written form: at some time it was written down. When did that happen?

Writing, in the fine new alphabet borrowed and improved from the Phoenicians, began again in Greece sometime after 750 B.C. We have a small but adequate number of inscriptions scratched on pottery or stone from the years before 700 B.C., most of them in verse. It must be remembered that any substantial literary work would have been written on papyrus, the ancient paper, imported from Egypt. The arid sands of Egypt itself will preserve papyri for millennia, and we possess a large number of portions of texts of Homer written on papyrus from the third century B.C. onwards; all come from Egypt, none from Greece, where the wet winters soon disintegrate them. So we have no very early written texts of Homer, from the centuries before the Greek conquest of Egypt, and little idea what they looked like.

It is a striking coincidence that the period in which writing was being introduced is also that to which we date the composition of the *Iliad*, and it is tempting to suppose that the two things are connected. Some have thought that the alphabet was introduced in order to write down the poems of Homer; others, less romantically, that it was the availability of writing which enabled a singer in the late stage of the tradition to create poems of extraordinary size and quality. Writing would make it possible to revise the work, to introduce cross-references, and to give the poems depth and meaning of a kind which would not be obvious at first hearing.

Another argument which is sometimes used is that the introduction of writing would of itself put an end to the oral tradition, at least in its creative form: the habit of reading weakens the memory, and access to a mass of written material dilutes the interest and spoils the taste for the old songs. In the long run that is probably true, and no doubt literacy played a part in the decline of the oral tradition. That decline is reflected in the change from the singers we see in Homer who chant their songs to an accompaniment on the lyre, to the 'rhapsodes' of later time, who lean on a staff, play no instrument, and explicitly reproduce the songs 'of Homer', instead of singing 'as the Muse set them on' (*Odyssey*, 8.73). But archaic Greece was not like the modern world, in which literacy immediately brings journalism and pulp fiction to produce a new and drastically altered taste in the societies which it enters. Its effects must have been far slower.

What is clear is that the *Odyssey*, like the *Iliad*, is the end product of an oral tradition. The things we have discussed in the last two sections are otherwise inexplicable. No literate poet, composing with pen and ink, would create such a style. But that does not show that the poem as we have it, our *Odyssey*, was itself created in that way. The scale of the two great epics is itself a very puzzling fact. We might imagine the audience of a bard wanting something much shorter, a song which could be performed and enjoyed at a sitting. The spicy tale of the guilty love of Ares and Aphrodite, the one song which Demodocus is allowed to sing to the Phaeacians without interruption, lasts a little over a hundred lines (8.266–369); that is not to be taken as the normal length of an heroic song, however, as the poet of the *Odyssey* wants to include a fairly short recital in the middle of a scene which is, after all, primarily concerned with building up to the self-revelation by Odysseus (9.19). Still, the picture of the position of singers in the *Odyssey* is of performers who are at the mercy of their audience and need to establish an ascendancy over them.

Very different, in important respects, is the position implied by a huge poem like the *Iliad* or the *Odyssey*. A singer who embarks on a song of such a size is evidently not expecting to be interrupted. We do not meet Odysseus until Book Five, that is until more than two thousand lines have passed; he does not reach Ithaca until Book Thirteen. To stop in the middle would be to miss the point altogether, and the singer, not the audience, is now in control. These poems both have a definite structure with a beginning and an end, and their creator must have envisaged their being performed, not just piecemeal, but as connected wholes. That meant performance over several days, and the loss by the audience of the power to choose a different theme tomorrow instead of going on with the *Odyssey*.

We do not know, and we never shall know, whether the poet of the *Iliad* dictated his poem to a scribe, or to a number of scribes simultaneously or in sequence, or whether he wrote it down himself, or used written notes to help with its construction. Perhaps he did none of these things but simply was a singer of exceptional powers, recognised as such by his audiences (for only with a great reputation, presumably, can he have induced them to trust him and to follow him through his enormous poem), who created a song which so impressed his hearers that they began to ask other singers not just for a song about Troy, or even for a song about Achilles, but for the *Iliad* of Homer. We do not know what are the limits of a great oral composer, and it is misleading to think that we can get at the truth by guessing at probabilities. It was not probable that a poet should appear in England, in the 1590s, who could write *Lear* and *Henry IV* and *A Midsummer Night's Dream*: both the extent of Shakespeare's superiority

over the other dramatists of the time, and the range of his out-
put, are far beyond anything which a prudent man would have
predicted for the English stage at the death of Christopher
Marlowe. It is not only what is likely which happens. In the case
of the *Odyssey* there is, moreover, the further point of the
influence on it of the *Iliad* (see section 13). A powerful
influence of one song on another may itself have implications
for the question of the form in which it was known to the
second composer.

What we can say is that the epics have a fundamentally oral
character, but that in scale and also in structure they are very
different from what we expect an oral song to be. They are
also, of course, outstanding in quality. Hitherto we have been
rather singling out oddities and difficulties. It is not to be
forgotten that the *Odyssey* is a great poem, which contains a
wide variety of tone and incidents, and passages of intense
poetry, as well as others which are comparatively unstressed.
It is wide-ranging, and its interests extend not only to heroes
and gods but also to women, to servants, to monsters. Its
complex and ambitious structure is, on the whole, carried
through with success. With the *Iliad* and *Odyssey* the oral
tradition reached an extraordinary culmination.

6. Alternative *Odysseys*?

We said in section 3 that a singer would handle a story differently on different occasions. He would sometimes hear
another bard's version of one of his own themes; he would go
on thinking about his own song; he would introduce a scene
or a motif from one song into another, and so on. There are
places in the *Odyssey* where different versions of a story do
seem to appear. For instance, the killing of Agamemnon by
the villainous Aegisthus, who succeeded in seducing his wife
and with her help murdered him on his triumphant return
from Troy, is told by the Old Man of the Sea in the following
terms: Aegisthus invited him to dinner and set upon his party
with a gang of twenty picked men:

And not one of Agamemnon's men was left, of those who followed him,
nor one of those of Aegisthus, but they were slain in the hall. (4.536–7)

But Agamemnon's own version is rather different. He tells Odysseus, in the Underworld, that

He slew me with the help of my wicked wife, inviting me to his house, as one kills an ox at a stall. So I died a most pitiful death, and my men were killed round me without pause like pigs slaughtered for a feast . . . there we lay, and the floor ran with blood.   (11.410–20)

One version imagines Agamemnon's men making a desperate fight of it, the other that they were slaughtered without resistance. Each is a possible story, the second perhaps the more powerful (the narration in Book Eleven does in fact go on to some very pathetic details). No doubt it was told both ways; both have left traces in the *Odyssey*.

That is a simple example of something peripheral to the poem. Closer to the heart of it lies the question of journeys both for Telemachus and perhaps also for Odysseus, different from those which they actually make. At one place in Book One, where the journey of Telemachus to Pylos and Sparta is outlined, some of the manuscripts contain two extra lines: Athena says

I shall escort him to Sparta and to sandy Pylos <and thence to Crete, to King Idomeneus, for he came home second of the bronze-corseleted Achaeans,> to seek for news of his father's homecoming.
                                             (1.93, 93a, 93b, 94)

The lines here put between angled brackets are not in most of the manuscripts, and of course they predict something which does not happen. Later in Book One we are told by an ancient commentator that at line 285 the great Homeric scholar Zenodotus (born about 325 B.C.) accepted a different reading from that of the main tradition: not

>Then go to Sparta, to fair-haired Menelaus

but

>Then go to Crete, to King Idomeneus   (1.285)

The variants are hard to account for as mere inventions, as they obviously contradict the plot, and it is tempting to think that there was at some time a version of the *Odyssey* in which both father and son did go to Crete. It might explain the remarkable number of stories told by Odysseus in which he claims to be a Cretan: to be on the run after killing the son of Idomeneus (13.256ff), to be the illegitimate son of a rich man (14.199ff), to be a prince (19.172ff). All this, and the raids on Egypt from Crete of which he boasts in Book Fourteen, might be episodes from another version of the poem, broken up and re-used in our *Odyssey*.

More interesting than a trip to Crete which does not, at least in our text, take place, is the visit of Odysseus to the land of the dead. There are several puzzles about this celebrated episode, not least the question why he has to make it at all; we shall return to that in section 11. At the moment it will be enough to observe that there are visible in Book Eleven two separate conceptions. The first is that of calling up the ghosts of the dead to a special place in the world of the living. Far away, in a dismal spot on the shores of the Ocean which surrounds the world, Odysseus digs a trench, performs some set ritual and prayers, and cuts the throats of two sheep so that their blood flows into the trench. Up flock the souls of the dead, young and old, men and women, and flutter squeaking about the trench and the blood: with drawn sword the hero must keep away all except those with whom he wishes to converse. If he allows them to drink of the blood, they are able to speak to him (11.23ff). That is a clear enough picture: it depicts what the Greeks called *nekyomantia*, necromancy, the consultation of selected ghosts for oracular purposes. Appropriately enough, the first ghost to be allowed to speak is that of the great Theban prophet Tiresias, whose horrific oracular utterances were to ring through such Attic tragedies as *Antigone* and *Oedipus the King*. Odysseus must stay where he is, by the blood; and the ghosts can only recognise him and speak to him when they have drunk some of it. But in the second half of Book Eleven it becomes increasingly clear that Odysseus is now down in the Underworld itself, mingling with the dead.

'Zeus-born son of Laertes, Odysseus of many plans', says the dead Achilles to him, 'rash man, what still greater exploit will you devise than this? How have you dared to come down to Hades, where the witless dead abide, the shadows of men outworn?'   (11.473–6)

Odysseus sees the great legendary sinners, who include characters like Tityos, stretched out on the ground, his liver gnawed by vultures, and Tantalus, who stands in a pool which recedes from his touch as he tries to drink. On his return Circe addresses Odysseus and his men: 'Rash men, who have gone down living into the house of Hades: twice dying ones, when other men die but once . . .' (12.21–2). Some people have tried to avoid the obvious conclusion by arguing that Odysseus remains at his post and observes these ghosts from that distance, but the idea is absurd in itself and contradicted by the language used.

It is clear that an original conception of one sort, which allowed for the hero's moving encounters with figures from his own past like his mother and King Agamemnon, has been overlaid with another, which is more exceptional, a greater heroic achievement. Many people, perhaps, could go in for necromancy, but only the very greatest of heroes could go down to the dead and return. It was the supreme hero, Heracles, who had done it: Heracles, who conquered both death and old age, who brought up Cerberus the Hound of Hell, and who in Greek belief was *alexikakos*, warder off of evils, who could be invoked for protection at any moment of danger or alarm. It is a high glorification for Odysseus to meet Heracles and be addressed by him as an equal: 'Unhappy man, in truth you too lead a life of suffering, the same as I endured beneath the rays of the sun . . .' (11.617–18). And if Odysseus was to go down to the dead, then he might well see the standard occupants of that world, Tantalus and the rest. That there has been an addition to a simpler older version is surely clear, but it does not follow that we can rediscover the older form by simply excising a number of lines, as scholars proposed in antiquity.

The most important of these questions relates to the central plot of the poem, the return and vengeance of Odysseus. The *Odyssey* tells the story in this way: for some years Penelope is beset in her house by a crowd of importunate Suitors. She keeps them at bay by the trick of the Web: 'Let me finish a shroud for Odysseus' old father Laertes, and then I will remarry.' So she said, and for three years she unwove by night what she wove by day, until at last she was discovered and finished her weaving perforce (2.93–110, 19.139–56, 24.127ff). Then, apparently, nothing happened; and later on Odysseus arrived, unrecognised by her. Not recognising him, she announced the contest with his great bow: whichever of the Suitors can string it most easily and shoot through the axes, him she will marry (19.577, 21.75). They all fail, and Odysseus gets the bow into his hands and begins his vengeance. Meanwhile Penelope is fast asleep, and when all is over she still cannot make up her mind to recognise the man who slew the Suitors as in truth Odysseus (23.1–240): an idea which makes possible the creation of a fine psychological scene.

That all seems straightforward. But there seem to be hints or traces of another story. In the last book one of the slain suitors tells Agamemnon this tale:

Penelope would neither say Yes nor No to remarriage, planning death and black fate for us. (She kept us off by means of the trick of the Web), but in the end she finished it perforce. And then an evil destiny brought Odysseus home from somewhere . . . He cunningly told his wife to set up the test of the bow for the Suitors . . .
(24.125–90)

That means, apparently, that (as we should expect) when Penelope found herself compelled to finish her weaving, then she had to start preparations for her marriage; and that she recognised Odysseus on his return and set up the test of the bow in complicity with him.

A good story, but different from that which we find in the text. Well; the last book is notoriously peculiar (see section 15) — or perhaps we can satisfy ourselves by supposing that this view of Penelope's action is only what the dead Suitors thought, a likely guess from their disgruntled point of view but in fact inaccurate. Unfortunately the matter is not quite so easily disposed of. In Book Twenty-One Penelope does in fact make not one but two speeches, urging that the bow

should be put into the hands of the disguised Odysseus
(21.311–42), a surprising thing if she really thinks him a
wandering beggar. Before that, in Book Nineteen, Odysseus
is told by Penelope that one of the maidservants will wash his
feet. He asks for an elderly woman, not a scornful young one,
thus ensuring that it will be done by his old nurse Eurycleia.
She sees the scar which he got on a boar-hunt as a young man:
there is a long account of the hunt and the scar, leading with
rising suspense to the moment when Eurycleia will find it
(19.317–467). The old woman drops his foot into the bowl,
upsetting it with a crash:

Joy and grief seized her heart at once, her eyes filled with tears, her
voice failed her. She touched Odysseus' cheek and said 'Indeed you
are Odysseus, my dear child, and I did not know my lord until I
touched you.' So she spoke, and she looked at Penelope, meaning
to tell her that her husband was come home: but Penelope could not
look at her or notice − Athena had turned her mind away'.

(19.471–9)

That is surely a very curious sequence of events. The foot-
washing, and particularly Odysseus' insistence that it should
be done by a woman old enough to remember his scar, seems
planned to lead up to a recognition; the length of the episode
suggests that the recognition should be a very important one;
Penelope is sitting by − and yet she remains unenlightened,
with the disconcertingly airy explanation that Athena did not
let her notice these noisy and dramatic events. At one time it
was the fashion to explain what has happened by the
hypothesis of another poem on the Odysseus story, which
told the tale in a different way and which was incorporated
in chunks into our *Odyssey*. More likely, perhaps, is the idea
that the situation was rather more fluid than that. The singer
had not only heard the story sung in different ways, he had
sung it in different ways himself. The oral performer tends to
think more, sometimes, of immediate effect than of the ab-
solute coherence of the long poem as a whole: the Eurycleia
episode is exciting, and the oddity of its conclusion, in a context which told the main story the other way, did not bother
the poet enough to make him exclude it.

The same is possibly true of the scene in Book Eighteen in which Penelope appears before the Suitors (18.158–301) dazzling them with her beauty – 'they all prayed to lie beside her in bed' – telling them that the way to woo a lady is not to consume her property but to bring presents.

They send off for rich gifts, and Odysseus is delighted at her skill in extracting them, 'while her heart was planning other things' (18.281–3). Again it has been argued that this scene suggests husband and wife in conscious collaboration. Otherwise, indeed, a husband might not be best pleased by such conduct in his wife. But the episode does have a function in our *Odyssey*. This is Penelope's first appearance to her husband, and he sees her as glamorous, irresistible, twisting the Suitors round her finger. This is her moment of glory, not as lachrymose grass widow or anxious mother but as triumphant beauty. The rather rough edges where it joins the main plot did not greatly worry the poet.

Our *Odyssey* emerges from a long tradition. At moments in it we catch glimpses of other possibilities and other versions, sometimes earlier, like the first conception of Book Eleven, sometimes perhaps later, like the idea of sending the heroes off to Crete (and, perhaps, replacing some of Odysseus' frankly supernatural or fairy-tale adventures with more conventional heroism, raiding Egypt), sometimes, for all we can tell, of the same age but a slightly different turn, like the two versions of the meeting of Odysseus and Penelope. Some oral epics tolerate really striking inconsistencies. In the *Nibelungenlied*, for instance, the name 'Nibelungs' is transferred, in the middle of the poem, from one set of characters to their enemies, with no explanation given; in the Irish epic of the *Tain* we find a princess marrying Cuchulainn after her death has been described. On the whole it must be said that our *Odyssey* is remarkably coherent, not only by the standards of oral epic, but also by those of any literature.

7. How the poem comes down to us

We saw in section 5 that mystery surrounds the original writing down of the Homeric poems. We do not even know whether, or in what form, they were written down by their creator or under his direction. Even if they were, they continued to be performed orally, and that meant that they were open to unpredictable forms of distortion. Singers naturally feel it their right to abbreviate, ornament, and develop a song in accordance with their own style, habits, and formulaic vocabulary. Against this, and the gloomy thoughts to which it might give rise for the authenticity of our text, stands the fact that in Greece there was present, as in most oral cultures there is not, the idea that one could ask not just for *a* song, but for *Homer*'s song. In that situation it is likely that there was some idea of truthfulness to a definitely conceived original. It is possible to preserve a text by oral transmission with extraordinary fidelity, if that is what, for some important reason, is wanted: the Rig Veda was so preserved for many centuries. But the motives of religious scruple which applied in India will not have been present in Homer's case.

We have some late and scattered evidence that in the sixth century B.C. an attempt was made to produce a 'standard' text of the *Iliad* and *Odyssey*. It is associated with the institution of regular public recitals of the whole of the poems at a great Athenian festival, the Panathenaea, held every four years. Athens at that time was ruled by 'tyrants', that is by one dominant family which had seized power by a combination of military backing and popular support. There are parallels in the Third World nowadays. The ruling family patronised literature and music, especially forms which could be spectacular and please the people: an organised recital of the great poems to the general public, which might otherwise never get to hear a good or complete performance, was an imaginative and popular move. For those recitals, which were performed by a number of singers in sequence, the authorities came up against the problem of an agreed text, if one singer were to be able to follow smoothly on from another.

There are certain traces of the Athenian dialect ('Attic Greek') in our text of Homer, and that combines with those scattered pieces of evidence to suggest that all extant texts go back ultimately to a copy or copies made in Athens, perhaps about 530 B.C. The existence of a written version would not by itself suffice to safeguard the text from change, especially before printing, and quotations from Homer in the fourth century often diverge from our text — usually not for the better. When we begin to get portions of copies on papyrus from the sands of Egypt, from the third century B.C., they offer texts which are marked by the presence of extra lines, sometimes in considerable numbers: generally they are repetitions of lines from elsewhere in the epics. Also they sometimes offer readings which attempt to simplify the text, get rid of difficulties, modernise spelling, and so on.

The second crucial event in the tradition of the poem is the rise of literary scholarship. In the fourth century B.C. there were learned men who worked on texts and wrote commentaries on the great poets, but this became professional and systematic at the Museum and Library of Alexandria about 300 B.C. The first Ptolemaic kings of Egypt were great collectors of books and of scholars, and the combination of both in one place made possible a new level of scholarly activity. First Zenodotus (born c. 325 B.C.) and then, at the end of the tradition, Aristarchus (c. 215–143 B.C.) produced texts which indicated lines which, on the evidence of manuscripts or on other grounds, they regarded as interpolated or corrupt. Aristarchus was famous in his lifetime, and we observe from about 150 B.C. that the 'wild' texts of Homer, bristling with extra lines, cease to be produced. The reading public was now aware that scholarly texts existed, and the book trade was producing a more or less standard article, which is essentially the text found in the medieval manuscripts of Homer and in our printed editions. It is not identical with that of the Alexandrian scholars, as we hear of their supporting different readings in some places, but it is affected by their work.

At some time the *Odyssey*, like the *Iliad*, was divided into twenty-four books. That number was evidently chosen

because there are twenty-four letters in the Greek alphabet,
and each book was often referred to simply by the name of
a letter. It is not likely that this arrangement is early, or that
the original singers conceived of their poems in that way. The
division is on the whole done sensibly, although one or two
books of the *Odyssey* are rather light: Books Six and Seven,
for instance, have only 671 verses between them, less than
some single books. It is noticeable that many books end with
night and sleep – thus for instance Books One, Two, Three,
Four, Five, and others. It is true that the action of the
Odyssey shows a definite tendency to divide into separate
days, each followed by an appearance of rose-fingered Dawn,
but perhaps there is also a feeling that an after-dinner song,
a single book, is now over, and it is time for bed. That would
be a possible way of reciting the poem: a book after dinner
for twenty-four nights.

Chapter 2

The poem

8. Summary

The *Odyssey* opens ten years after the fall of Troy. The Trojan War was caused by the crime of the Trojan prince Paris, who abducted from Sparta the beautiful Helen, wife of King Menelaus, whose brother Agamemnon of Mycenae, 'king of men', led a great expedition against Troy. Prominent heroes on the Greek side were Achilles, son of the sea-goddess Thetis; the aged Nestor; Ajax; Diomedes, and Odysseus. After ten years of siege Achilles killed Hector the Trojan champion. Achilles himself was killed, but through the trick of the Wooden Horse a select force of Greeks entered the city and took it. At the sack of Troy some Greeks, notably the minor hero Ajax 'the lesser', committed crimes against the gods, especially their own patron goddess Athena; she raised storms against them on their way home, and some were lost. Agamemnon, on his triumphant return, was murdered by his wife and her lover Aegisthus.

Ten years later Odysseus has not returned to his western island of Ithaca. In his absence his wife Penelope is beset by a crowd of suitors, the young nobles of Ithaca and neighbouring islands, whom she has kept at bay by clever tactics. They are now trying to wear down Penelope and her son Telemachus, who is about twenty, by feasting in the house and consuming their substance. Meanwhile Odysseus is stranded on a remote island, detained by the amorous nymph Calypso; and at home the situation is approaching a climax.

Book 1 Our subject is the wily wanderer Odysseus and his hard adventures. Athena asks Zeus, as the gods are assembled on Olympus, why he has forgotten Odysseus. Zeus replies that the anger of the sea god Poseidon still pursues the hero who blinded the god's son, the Cyclops Polyphemus. But now Poseidon is away, and the hero's return can begin. Athena goes down to Ithaca in disguise and encourages the despairing Telemachus: he should summon a general meeting and try to mobilise public opinion against the Suitors; and he should go in quest of news of his father, to King Nestor in Pylos and King Menelaus in Sparta. For the first time Telemachus speaks aggressively both to the Suitors and to Penelope.

Book 2 Telemachus summons the assembly, and a series of speeches are made. The Suitors are defiant, and despite some encouraging speeches and omens public opinion is not roused to intervene. Telemachus secretly makes preparations for his journey. Athena, in the form of the man Mentor, has got a ship ready, and they leave by night.

Book 3 Telemachus comes to Pylos to Nestor, oldest and wisest of the Greeks who were at Troy. Stories are told of the Return from Troy of other heroes, especially Menelaus and Agamemnon; but Nestor has not heard news of Odysseus for ten years. He sends his son Pisistratus to go with Telemachus to Sparta.

Book 4 Telemachus and Pisistratus come to the palace of Menelaus, who is celebrating a double wedding. They are entertained by Menelaus and Helen, a *grande dame* and by no means in disgrace. Menelaus tells the long story of his adventure off the coast of Egypt: the Old Man of the Sea told him that Odysseus was detained by Calypso on a distant island. The Suitors learn with chagrin of Telemachus' departure, and plan to ambush and kill him at sea on his way back. Penelope also learns of it and is distressed.

Book 5 The gods on Olympus again. Hermes the messenger is sent to tell Calypso to let Odysseus go. She expresses bitterness but obeys: after offering him immortality with her, an offer which is tactfully declined, she gives him tools and wood and he builds a boat. He sails for seventeen days. Poseidon spies him and wrecks his boat in a storm. He struggles ashore naked in the land of the Phaeacians.

Book 6 The Phaeacian princess Nausicaa and her maids wash clothes and play ball on the shore. Odysseus throws himself on her mercy and is accepted, clothed, and told to go to the palace of her father, King Alcinous.

Book 7 Odysseus implores the help of Alcinous and his queen, Arete. He tells them a short version of his story but conceals his identity. He evades Alcinous' hint that he might marry Nausicaa.

Book 8 Odysseus is entertained by the Phaeacians. The blind singer Demodocus sings of the Trojan War and Odysseus' role in it: the hero weeps. The young men show their skill at athletics. Odysseus is reluctant to join in, but when rudely challenged shows his prowess. Demodocus sings the tale of the amours of Ares and Aphrodite, and again of Troy. Odysseus weeps and is again asked: Who are you?

Book 9   The hero reveals his name and tells his story, starting after the Sack of Troy with twelve ships. First he raided the Cicones in Thrace, then he was blown far off course to the land of the Lotus-Eaters and to the island of the Cyclopes. Curiosity and greed led him and his companions into the cave of the Cyclops Polyphemus. He extricated himself by blinding the monster and by the tricks of calling himself Noman and clinging under the belly of a ram. When he rashly revealed his true name, Polyphemus prayed for vengeance to his father Poseidon.

Book 10   They come to the floating island of the god Aeolus, who at their departure gives Odysseus a leather bag containing all the winds except the favourable West Wind. While Odysseus sleeps, his sailors open the bag: they are blown back to Aeolus, who refuses to have any more to do with them. They come to the Laestrygonians, who turn out to be ogres and destroy eleven of the ships with their crews. The surviving ship comes to the island of Circe, who turns some of the sailors into pigs but is subdued by Odysseus. After a year of love, the hero asks to leave: Circe tells him he must first visit the dead and get instructions from the dead prophet Tiresias.

Book 11   They call up the dead in a sinister and remote spot. Tiresias gives instructions, and tells Odysseus of the travels he must still make after the end of the *Odyssey*. The ghosts appear of Odysseus' mother, of Agamemnon and Achilles, and others. Odysseus sees, in the Underworld, the punishments of the great sinners.

Book 12   Circe tells them how to go. They pass the monster Scylla and the whirlpool Charybdis and come to the island with the sacred cattle of the Sun, which they have been warned not to touch. Driven by hunger, they slaughter and eat some. The Sun complains to Zeus, who destroys the ship with a thunderbolt. Odysseus alone survives and on the mast of his ship drifts to Calypso's island.

Book 13   The Phaeacians land Odysseus, deeply asleep, with Alcinous' rich gifts on the beach of Ithaca. Athena comes along, disguised as a young man. Odysseus tries to deceive her but fails: she expresses her affection for him, and they plan the campaign against the Suitors. She disguises him as a decrepit beggar.

Book 14   Odysseus goes to the hut of the loyal swineherd Eumaeus. He entertains Eumaeus with invented tales about himself.

Book 15   Telemachus in Sparta. Farewells from Menelaus and Helen. Telemachus evades the tedious hospitality of Nestor and sails for home, picking up a seer, Theoclymenus by name, who is on the run. On Ithaca, Eumaeus tells his own life-story to Odysseus. Telemachus avoids the Suitors' ambush.

Book 16   Telemachus goes to Eumaeus' hut. Odysseus reveals himself to his son and impresses on him the need for self-control in the struggle with the Suitors. The ambush ship returns; the Suitors hold an inconclusive debate on what to do next.

Book 17 Telemachus returns to his house and encounters Penelope. Eumaeus brings Odysseus to the house. They meet the wicked goatherd Melanthius, who serves and supports the Suitors: he insults Odysseus. As they approach the house, the old dog Argus recognises his master and dies. Odysseus begs for food from the Suitors. Antinous, a leading Suitor, throws a footstool at him.

Book 18 The boastful poltroon Irus, a professional beggar, insults Odysseus: in a boxing match Odysseus knocks him out. Penelope comes in to show herself to the Suitors and extract handsome presents from them. Odysseus is delighted. The disloyal maidservant Melantho insults him; he has the best of an exchange of insults with Eurymachus, a leading Suitor, who throws a footstool at him.

Book 19 Odysseus and Telemachus remove the weapons from the hall: Athena lights their way. Melantho insults Odysseus again. Odysseus and Penelope begin a lengthy conversation. He convinces her that he entertained Odysseus years ago and tells her that he is now not far away, on his way home, but she will not be convinced. The old nurse Eurycleia washes his feet and recognises him by a scar as Odysseus. Penelope tells him a dream and describes the test of the bow, which she will set to the Suitors the next night.

Book 20 Odysseus, lying awake, finds self-mastery difficult. Omens portend success for him. The loyal oxherd Philoetius appears. A third Suitor, Ctesippus, throws an ox-foot at Odysseus. The Suitors are overcome with crazy laughter: the seer Theoclymenus sees them as marked out for death.

Book 21 Penelope fetches the bow of Odysseus and announces the test: stringing the bow and shooting through the axes. The Suitors in turn try to string the bow but fail. Odysseus reveals his identity to Eumaeus and Philoetius. All the Suitors fail except Antinous, who postpones his turn. Odysseus succeeds, over their opposition, in getting hold of the bow, Penelope being sent away from the hall; he strings it and shoots through the axes.

Book 22 Odysseus shoots Antinous and reveals himself to the astonished Suitors. With Telemachus, Eumaeus and Philoetius he begins to destroy them. Melanthius brings some of the suits of armour back to the Suitors, but he is caught in the act. When Odysseus' arrows run out he too puts on armour, and the battle is finished with spears. All the Suitors are killed. The disloyal maidservants are hanged and Melanthius gruesomely punished.

Book 23 Eurycleia informs Penelope, who refuses to believe that this is Odysseus. After a scene of fencing between husband and wife, Odysseus reveals himself in response to her trick instruction to move his bed. He tells her his true story, and the two are united at last in love.

Book 24 Hermes shepherds the souls of the Suitors down to the Underworld. They meet Agamemnon and Achilles and converse with them. Agamemnon describes the funeral of Achilles at Troy. Odysseus goes to his poor old father Laertes, who is living rough. After a false story, he reveals himself. The kinsmen of the Suitors meet and plan vengeance. Athena and Zeus plan lasting peace on Ithaca. There is a skirmish, in which a few of the kinsmen are killed: Athena makes peace.

9. Translating Homer

'Traduttori traditori', 'translators, traitors', says the Italian proverb. To translate poetry at all inevitably involves loss, and what is lost is all too often the specifically poetic element. The special difficulties about translating Homer are evident: the *Odyssey* is ancient, embodying ideas and uses of language which are remote from ours; it is in a grand style; and, above all, there is nothing like it in English. At the beginning of Greek literature stand two great poems composed in the oral style, which were never lost to sight but always continued to be read, admired, and imitated. English literature does not contain anything like that: *Beowulf* was unknown for centuries, and when it was rediscovered it seemed to be in another language. If such works did exist in English, then in principle a talented translator could render Homer in their style. The eighteenth century was the great age of translations from Greek and Latin into English, and at that time men like Dryden could render Latin verse with a panache and brilliance unattainable to later writers. Dryden's *Juvenal*, and even his *Virgil*, are notably more like the originals than Pope's *Iliad* and *Odyssey* are like Homer, largely for the reason that Homer is so different from anything to be found in English, while the rhetoric of Latin poetry does resemble that of Dryden in his English poems.

The translator of Homer is immediately confronted by the problem of the repeated epithets and the formulaic expressions. Is Odysseus to be constantly called 'much enduring crafty Odysseus'? 'To him in answer spoke prudent Telemachus': is the translation to be regularly dotted with such lines? Worse, what is to be done about phrases like 'the holy might of Telemachus', *hierē īs Tēlemachoio*, or 'the holy strength of Alcinous', *hieron menos Alkinooio*, several times used to mean 'Telemachus' and 'Alcinous'? These phrases are in all probability of great antiquity, related both to Near Eastern poetry and to early notions of the *mana* or magical power of kings, but for Homer they are no more, apparently, than stylistically elevated periphrases. E. V. Rieu, in the Penguin Classic translation, regularly says, when Odysseus is addressed as 'Zeus-born son of Laertes, Odysseus of many plans', only 'addressing Odysseus by his royal titles'. That is perhaps a possible solution, at least sometimes. The trouble is, in general terms, that to omit all these repeated lines and words removes an important ingredient from Homer, while to render them all into English seems to give them more emphasis than they would really have received, in an oral tradition which took them for granted and reposed in them for a moment as they went by. There can, then, be no perfectly satisfactory solution, as it is impossible to produce on a modern reader the same effect as these formulae had on their original audience.

The early translators of Homer took it for granted that he should be rendered into verse. Of the two celebrated verse translations, that of George Chapman, memorably praised by Keats in his sonnet 'On First Looking into Chapman's Homer', has all the exuberance, and all the quaintness, of the Elizabethan period. His version of the *Odyssey* is a finer performance than his *Iliad*. It contains delightful couplets, but as a whole it must be said to be not very like the original. Alexander Pope's translation of Homer, the work which made him wealthy and independent, is one of the unread masterpieces of English literature. Its defects are obvious. Pope imposes on the varied rhythms of Homer the unchanging exactness of his rhyming couplets. He points up all the rhetorical touches that are there, and adds many more that are not. He extends passages and chops off details with sovereign freedom. He sometimes dislikes the simplicity or 'lowness' of Homer and raises his utterance to a consistent level of dignity appropriate to eighteenth-century gentlemen. Here is a passage from Book Ten, the transformation by Circe of the sailors:

> But venom'd was the bread, and mix'd the bowl,
> With drugs of force to darken all the soul:
> Soon in the luscious feast themselves they lost
> And drank oblivion of their native coast.
> Instant her circling wand the goddess waves,
> To hogs transforms them, and the sty receives.
> No more was seen the human form divine;
> Head, face, and members, bristle into swine:
> Still cursed with sense, their minds remain alone,
> And their own voice affrights them when they groan.
>
> (10.235–44)

The splendid rhythm and life of that style, which Pope can keep up amazingly, must impress us. It was reached at a certain cost: 'in the luscious feast themselves they lost', 'drank oblivion', 'the human form divine', 'still cursed with sense', and the whole of the last line: all this is essentially added by Pope to the barer and less rhetorical narrative of Homer. The last line, particularly, is in the style of Ovid and utterly un-Homeric.

Yet, after all, Pope's version is a poem, and a fine one; and if a Frenchman, say, were to ask us whether he would get more impression of Shakespeare from a translation into French prose or from a free rendering into good French verse, it would not be obvious, surely, that the former is the right answer. Homer is poetry. The *Odyssey* contains, as well as formulaic phrases, many of the linguistic devices which we think of as characteristically poetic. There is sound-painting, for instance in the description of Charybdis, full of rugged and onomatopoeic verbs and harsh consonants:

> ē toi hot *exemeseie*, lebēs hōs en puri pollōi
> pās' *anamormūreske kukōmene, hupsose* d'*achnē*
> *akroisi skopeloisin* ep' *amphoteroisin epipten.*
> all' hot' *anabroxeie* thalassēs halmuron hūdōr,
> pas' entosthe *phaneske kukōmene*, amphi de petrē
> deinon *bebrūchei* . . .
>
> (12.237–42)

> (When she vomited forth, like a pot on a great fire she seethed
> and stirred to her depths, and the spray on high fell on the top-
> most rocks on both sides; but when she sucked in the salt sea-
> water, she was revealed within, swirling to her depths, and all
> round the rock roared fearfully . . .)

The k's, s's and p's in this passage (compare 5.401f) echo the
fearful sounds of the maelstrom.

At an opposite stylistic extreme, the insulting maid Melantho finds biting expression for her taunts to Odysseus. 'Are
you unhinged by beating Irus the vagabond?' she asks:

> mē tis toi tacha Īrou ameinōn allos anastēi,
> hos tis s' amphi karē kekopōs chersi stibareisi
> dōmatos ekpempsēisi phoruxās haemati pollōi   (18.334–6)

> (Take care that a stronger man than Irus doesn't face you,
> who will punch you about the head with powerful fists and
> throw you out of the house covered in blood.)

The alliteration of t, a, k, p, gives shape and thrust to the
gibe.

That is only to say, what is obvious enough, that the
Odyssey really is a poem, whose effects are intimately connected with the exact words used. A paraphrase in prose cannot be quite like that. And yet it is very hard to produce a
translation into a modern verse idiom of such a long poem,
or into any verse idiom of a poem whose range, of subject-
matter and of style, is so wide. The version by Richmond
Lattimore is the work of a good scholar. It is said to be in
'free six-beat lines'; it is not always easy to hear those six
beats, and the effect to my ear often resembles prose, while
the style wavers at times between literal translation, archaism,
and the colloquial. A better example of a translation into
verse of a modern idiom is that by Robert Fitzgerald (New
York, 1961), into very free blank verse.

What then of prose translations? The Penguin version by
E. V. Rieu is readable, and it has been read by millions of
people. Its aim was to translate not so much the words as the
'original effect' as he judged it to have been. What trips one
up, I think, is less the occasional bold piece of substitution —
for the phrase (admittedly a difficult one) 'What speech has

passed the barrier of your teeth!' Rieu writes 'I never thought to hear such words from you' − as the general stylistic level. When Odysseus meet Heracles among the dead.

> One look was enough to tell Heracles who I was, and he greeted me in mournful tones. 'Unhappy man!' he exclaimed, after reciting my titles . . .

A closer translation would run something like this:

> He knew me at once, when his eyes beheld me, and with a groan he spoke to me winged words: 'Zeus-born son of Laertes, Odysseus of many plans, o luckless man . . .'

The whole stylistic level of Rieu is completely different, and the sense of formality of utterance is lost.

A translation which keeps more of the manner and level of the original is that of Walter Shewring (Oxford, 1980). Naturally something is lost in the turn from verse to prose, but Shewring is skilful at avoiding stylistic lapses and disconcerting irregularities of level. He also includes a thoughtful essay on the problems of Homeric translation. A reader will get from his version a good sense of the dignity and consistency of the original. It is interesting to compare it with the essay *On Translating Homer* by Matthew Arnold, which criticises some nineteenth-century translations and offers his own thoughts on the matter: Arnold's criticisms of other people's versions are penetrating, his own attempts to improve on them less satisfactory. In addition to a reliable prose version, a reader may be helped to recapture some of the lost poetic glitter of the *Odyssey* by reading some sections in Pope's verse translation. Between the two one can get a sense of the quality of the original.

10. Shape and unity

The essential plot of the *Odyssey* is very simple. The hero returns in the nick of time and delivers his wife from her importunate Suitors by killing them, thus regaining wife, house, and kingdom. It is one − the final one − of the return stories, a number of which were versified in another early epic, later than the *Odyssey*, of unknown authorship called *Nostoi* (*Homecomings*), describing the various adventures of the Achaean chieftains coming back from Troy.

The *Odyssey* has been expanded to a great size. The influence of the *Iliad* (see section 13) was no doubt of prime importance here, as the *Odyssey* poet embarked on a process of creative imitation and rivalry, to produce an epic of scale comparable with that great poem. In the early poetic tradition one of the formulaic phrases for Odysseus seems to have been 'Telemachus' father' (*Iliad* 2.260, 4.354). That suggests that something was known about Telemachus, that there was some story about him. It is unlikely, however, that what was known included anything like the journey of Telemachus in Books Three and Four of our *Odyssey*, as that journey comes to nothing as a separate tale – no achievement, no fighting, just sailing home again – and has a meaning only within the monumental Odysseus-poem. It seems likely, then, that Telemachus' trip was created for the *Odyssey*, and that means that the first four books, and Telemachus' leave-taking from Sparta in Book Fifteen, were all created for the poem by the great poet whose total conception the extended *Odyssey* represents.

Two important threads for the *Odyssey* are visible here. One is the promotion of Telemachus to an important role in the poem. Instead of the hero standing alone, he is to be supported by his son. Since the son has, by definition, been incapable of any heroic enterprise up to now, the *Odyssey* can show us the young man in the process of achieving adult status, asserting himself for the first time both with the Suitors and with his mother. The Suitors immediately draw the conclusion that things cannot go on in their present agreeable way once Telemachus has started acting like a man, and that he must be killed. That adds to the tension of the poem with the ambush laid for him, and in addition increases the guilt of the Suitors: for this anxiously moral poet that has the bonus of justifying their drastic punishment.

The second thread is the desire to complete the story of the *Iliad*, to bring into the *Odyssey* the glamorous and exciting people familiar from that poem, and to describe their subsequent fates. The ill-starred return of Agamemnon, with the treachery of his wife and his avenging by his son, is repeatedly brought in as a foil and a warning to Odysseus and Telemachus. We also meet Nestor, Menelaus and Helen: delightful vignettes, in which Telemachus learns how to mix at his ease with his peers. We are shown some comedy of manners (especially between Menelaus and Helen, see section 17), and some good stories are told. The tale of Agamemnon is explicitly a model for Odysseus; that of Menelaus is also made parallel with the main plot of the *Odyssey*. He too is stranded on a distant island, helped by a goddess, forced to disguise himself as an animal − Menelaus in the skin of a seal (4.440ff), recalls Odysseus under the belly of a ram (9.424) − forced to hold on and dissemble and endure (4.447), delayed in his return by acts of neglect towards the gods (4.472).

Other stories of Troy, too, are skilfully brought in. Helen tells us how Odysseus entered Troy in disguise, an episode which looks forward to his disguised presence, in the second half of the poem, in his own house (4.239–64). Menelaus replies by telling of Odysseus inside the Trojan Horse. Helen went round the Horse, imitating the voice of the wives of several of the heroes inside. The others wanted to yield to this temptation and reveal themselves; Odysseus restrained them. We see the parallel with his restraint of himself and of Telemachus when tempted to self-revelation on Ithaca. Odysseus seized one hero, who was about to cry out, by the throat − as he seized his old nurse Eurycleia, when she was about to reveal his identity (4.277–8, 19.480–1).

The trip to the Underworld, which is not very strongly anchored to the plot by anything Odysseus needs there, also allowed the Iliadic persons to appear again: Agamemnon and Achilles and Odysseus' great enemy Ajax, still unreconciled beyond the grave. Achilles speaks movingly of death, and also speaks of his old father Peleus: in his son's absence he is probably being deprived of livelihood and dishonoured. 'If only I could come back just for a minute, the hero that I was at Troy − that would put a stop to them', says Achilles

(11.497). Again it is clear how much all these stories are adapted to their position in the *Odyssey*: several people utter the same wish for Odysseus, that he might reappear, armed, 'such as he was when −' (1.255, 3.233, 4.341). Achilles is shown yearning to return and deliver his family, like Odysseus.

The conception of starting the poem with Odysseus off-stage for the first four books was a bold one. Not only did it involve technical difficulties in handling and uniting two strands of narrative, it also risked the first appearance of the hero being an anti-climax. In the first four books Odysseus is constantly mentioned: he is in everyone's thoughts. On Ithaca life has been in a kind of limbo for twenty years, with no public assemblies since Odysseus left. Old Nestor, a well-informed man, thinks constantly of Odysseus but has not set eyes on him for ten years. A long journey brings us to Sparta, where Menelaus tells us that long ago and far away he was told by a god that Odysseus was held on an island by a nymph, without a ship. From that tremendous climax of remoteness the hero must somehow return.

The decision that the *Odyssey* should be set ten years after the fall of Troy − the figure strongly recalling the ten years of war at Troy which have elapsed before the *Iliad* − meant that most of Odysseus' adventures would have to be told retrospectively. It would be highly anti-climactic to narrate all that after the killing of the Suitors and the dissipating of tension, so a place needed to be found where the stories could be unpacked at leisure. Doubtless also the poet preferred, as Aristotle remarked, to let Odysseus himself, rather than the primary narrator, vouch for the truth of those tales; they are full of fantastic creatures, far beyond what the poet tells us in his own person, and if the audience is sceptical of the truth of some of them, why, everyone knows that sailors tell tall stories.

The Phaeacians provide the setting for the tales. They are men, but remote from ordinary humanity and close to the gods: they serve as a transition between the fantasy world of the tales and the human world of Ithaca. The poet is explicit about their early history (6.1–2) and also about the reason why there are no marvellous Phaeacian ships to bring home shipwrecked mariners nowadays (13.125–87): that may suggest that they are largely the poet's own creation. Among the Phaeacians the pace of events is leisurely, and in Book Seven especially very little happens. They are seen with a certain irony, these privileged people, who live comfortably, never have to fight, and excel at 'swift running, and sailing; and always we love the feast, and music, and dance, and changes of clothes, and hot baths, and bed' (8.246–9). No wonder that among them the queen wears the trousers. She is honoured by everybody as no other wife on earth is honoured: she settles disputes among men, and it is to her that Odysseus should address himself (7.66–77).

The adventures are in themselves timeless and placeless, belonging to Sinbad the Sailor as much as to Odysseus. Somehow they have become attached to the name of one of the heroes who fought at Troy, in a definite historical context. An effort has been made to arrange them in a coherent and morally intelligible order (see section 14), especially in terms of obedience to the gods and resolute endurance. Apart from their intrinsic interest, they are needed in order to keep the Odysseus of Books Thirteen to Twenty-One, who does very little that is heroic, accepts humiliations, and at moments looks like a real beggar rather than a hero, in our minds as a man of truly great deeds.

The second half of the poem develops some new notes, with the hut of Eumaeus, lovingly dwelt upon, resembling pastoral rather than epic – humble meals, dogs, the care of animals, simple folk. In the palace of Odysseus things move more slowly than we expect, and there is a tendency for things to happen more than once: Suitors throw things at Odysseus, Melantho insults him, the hero shakes his head in grim silence. There is a gathering of pace, with the intensity of Odysseus' conversation with Penelope in Book Nineteen, the tense expectation at the opening of Twenty, and the bringing-out of the bow in Twenty-One, but at moments the reader has almost the feeling that the fluent poet is producing variations on his themes for their own sake, in love with his characters and reluctant to terminate his plot. The killing of the Suitors and the reunion of husband and wife (see section 17) are handled with great brilliance, and if events after that exhibit certain oddities and signs of being less than organic (see section 15), they do tie up the ends of the story and bring the poem to a reasonably satisfactory conclusion.

And the whole poem is pervaded and held together by a very explicit theory of justice and of divine behaviour, discussed more fully in section 16. Zeus is ultimately responsible for the protection of the helpless, beggars and suppliants and good kings in distress. All that happens in the *Odyssey* is, as far as possible, made to illustrate that conception. Sinners are, in the end, punished; the final triumph of Odysseus is a triumph for goodness over evil. We are far from the bleaker vision of the last Book of the *Iliad*. Zeus accepts, in his first words of the poem, the challenge of devising manifest justice (1.31ff): the destruction of the Suitors is proclaimed, by all the characters, as its satisfying fulfilment (22.411, 23.63, 24.36).

11. The epic style: grandeur and realism

The most frequently mentioned feature of Homeric style in antiquity is its elevation. Epic and tragedy were regarded as the highest forms of poetry, which presented suffering and death in noble language and illuminated in a worthy manner the nature of the world and the dealings of the gods with mankind. The stories are set in a past which is felt to be both different and special. Heroes then were greater and stronger; heroines were beloved by gods and bore them god-like children; above all, the gods intervened visibly in events, mixing with men and speaking to them. Heroic myth in high poetry makes the world transparent, allowing us to see the divine workings which in ordinary events are concealed. That is why not only epic but also tragedy is concerned with those myths: they allow a privileged insight into the hidden patterns of life.

Such actors and such events needed a style and diction to

match. The style of Homer is not pompous or slow-moving; its oral and formulaic origin tends to make each line a unit in itself, often extended by run-on (enjambement), but radically different in movement from, say, the opening lines of *Paradise Lost*, although Milton of course has the Homeric openings in mind:

> Of Man's First Disobedience, and the Fruit
> Of that forbidden Tree, whose mortal taste
> Brought Death into the World, and all our woe,
> With loss of *Eden*, till one greater Man
> Restore us, and regain the blissful Seat,
> Sing Heav'nly Muse . . .

No verb until line six, and no full stop until line sixteen. Such solemn density is not Homeric. The elevation of Homer is achieved by a number of devices: the recurrent and dignified epithets, the general avoidance of vagueness in expression, the firm control of varying pace and movement, the objective tone in which events are narrated, the exclusion of 'low' words and motives. This last must however immediately be qualified. Homer describes a dog dying on a dung-hill, full of fleas (17.297–300); he tells us about a punch-up between two beggars with a couple of blood-puddings as a prize (18.43–116); he retails the insults of an offensive servant – 'Here's one bit of bad news bringing another! True enough, God makes birds of a feather flock together. Where are you taking this man, you miserable swineherd? – This pest of a beggar, who will stand and rub his back on the doorposts—' (17.217–21). Napoleon, always on his dignity, was shocked by the punch-up with the beggar Irus, and none of those passages, which could easily be multiplied, can be imagined in the *Aeneid*, or in Milton, or in Racine. Homer is not afraid of the natural, and he is confident that his style will raise the humble rather than being dragged down by it.

Here is an unstressed passage of the *Odyssey*, to show how routine events are handled in a style which is essentially simple. It describes the embarkation of Telemachus for his journey:

They brought all the gear on the well-benched ship and set it down, as the dear son of Odysseus had told them. Then Telemachus went on board the ship; Athena went first and sat down in the stern. Beside her Telemachus took his seat. The men untied the stern-ropes, went aboard, and sat at their benches. Grey-eyed Athena sent them a following breeze, a fresh west wind, sounding over the wine-dark sea. Telemachus urged on his men, ordering them to handle the tackling, and they obeyed the order. They stepped the mast of pine in the hollow mast-box and set it up, and fastened it to the forestays, and lowered the white sails with plaited leather ropes. The wind bellied out the middle of the sail, and the water resounded loudly, foaming round the keel as the ship went on. They fastened the tackle, and in the swift black ship they set up bowls brimming with wine, and poured libations to the immortal gods who live forever, but most of all to the grey-eyed daughter of Zeus. All through the night and the dawn the ship went cleaving her way.   (2.414–34)

Such a passage is not meant to surprise, except in as far as a midnight launch was unusual (ancient sailors in those narrow and dangerous seas generally preferred to beach their ships at night). The 'wine-dark sea' is a traditional English rendering of the Greek phrase *oinopa ponton*, literally 'the wine-faced sea', which probably refers to the sparkling bubbles on the surface, resembling those seen as one raises a beaker of newly poured wine: the ancients did not drink out of glass. In any case it is a regular Homeric phrase, and the fact that this time it is dark and the sea visible in an unusual way makes no difference. The two lines describing the sail bellying and the water resounding round the keel recur identically at *Iliad* 1.481–2, yet here they are beautifully appropriate, and the poet was content without trying to outdo them. The point of the passage as a whole is its peace and order, a welcome relief after the disorder and conflict on Ithaca. Outside the claustrophobic setting of Odysseus' house there is the unchanging world of nature: the anarchy of the Suitors is contrasted with the unchanging discipline of sailors. And we contemplate the ship, manned by its obedient crew, moving on through the darkness, amid the sounds of wind and water, natural yet (in this heroic world) god-given. The objective manner and the recurrent phrases, which suggest the regularity of it all, fit effortlessly with such effects.

That passage can be compared with another, more intense, also describing the launching of a ship by night. Odysseus, after all the perils he described in Books Nine to Twelve, has finally reached the point where the Phaeacians will take him home. We have just heard how he 'kept turning his head to the blazing sun, yearning for it to set', as he waited for the evening, when they are to sail; he was as glad to see the sun go down as a man who has all day been ploughing and who now heads for his supper, 'and his knees tremble as he goes' (13.28–35). A bed is laid out for the hero in the stern:

He came on board and lay down in silence, and the crew sat each at his bench in order, and they untied the hawser from the stone capstan. Then swinging back they began to fling up the salt water with the oar; and on his eyelids there fell sweet sleep, unbroken and delightful, most like to death. As for the ship: as when four stallions draw a chariot on flat ground, all lunging together beneath the blow of the lash, and rising high they speedily make their journey – even so would her stern rise, and behind her seethed the heaving wave of the ever roaring sea. The ship ran steadily on; not even a hawk could keep pace, the swiftest of flying things, so fast was her run as she cleft the waves of the sea, bearing a man like to the gods in planning, whose heart had endured much suffering in time past, threading his way through warring men and cruel sea; now he slept deeply, forgetting all he had suffered. When the star rose that is brightest, which especially comes to announce the light of early-rising Dawn, at that time the sea-going ship touched at the island.   (13.75–95)

At once we observe that the purely standard features of launching and sailing have been much compressed. The elements of normality are still there – the ropes which must be untied before the ship can leave, the oarsmen flinging up the salt water – but the focus is on Odysseus and his sleep. As so often in the Homeric poems, at a high point in the narrative the words and phrases used for the action do not change, but special novelty and emphasis are introduced by a striking comparison (the chariot bouncing over the plain) and by an unusual point of reference (the hawk in flight). The poet pauses in his narration to linger in pity and sympathy on the sleeping figure of his hero, released for a short time from tribulations past and future. In so deep a sleep he can cross from the non-human world of the Phaeacians and the

Wanderings and return to real life and a fresh set of problems. 'A man whose heart had endured much suffering' in war and on the sea strongly recalls the opening words of the poem – a man of many wanderings and much suffering. It is hard not to see a conscious echo here, and a hint that this is a new start for the hero: so striking a passage, at such a point in the poem, makes it plausible that an oral audience would have been expected to catch that echo.

Another high point in the poem, this time in an active rather than a passive mood, is the moment when Odysseus finally gets the great bow into his hands. Unhurried, he turns it and inspects it, in case it has been gnawed by worms: the Suitors jeer – 'I suppose he's got bows like that at home – perhaps he's planning to make one –'

So spoke the Suitors: but Odysseus of many plans, as soon as he had handled the bow and examined it thoroughly – as when a man skilled in lyre-playing and in song effortlessly stretches a new string round the peg, fastening the twisted sheep-gut at either end – even so, without effort, did Odysseus string the great bow. Then he took it in his hand and tried the string: it sang out sweetly, like the voice of a swallow. The Suitors were greatly vexed, and the colour of all of them changed. Zeus thundered loudly, giving an omen, and noble much-enduring Odysseus rejoiced at the sign sent him by the son of Cronos of the crooked counsels. He took a swift arrow which lay by on the table, naked: the rest were within the hollow quiver, those arrows which soon the Achaeans would sample. He held it on his forearm and drew back string and notched arrow end, sitting in his chair as he was, and aiming straight before him he let the arrow fly, and of all the axes he missed not one handle tip: the arrow with heavy bronze point went through them all to the door. And Odysseus said to Telemachus: 'Your guest who sits in your house has not shamed you, Telemachus: I have not missed that mark, nor did I labour long to string the bow; my strength is still unchanged, not as the Suitors in contempt reproached me. Now it is time for a supper to be got ready for the Achaeans while it is light, and then for play, with song and lyre – they are the ornaments of the feast.'
(21.404–30)

What is emphasised here is the ease and smoothness with which the hero does what nobody else could do at all. The comparison with a singer who strings his lyre is not only vivid but also pregnant. Repeatedly Odysseus has been compared to a professional singer: Alcinous actually said to him that he 'told his tale like a singer, well and skilfully', and it holds the Phaeacians entranced; Eumaeus, too, gazed at him 'as a man gazes at a singer' (11.368, 13.2, 14.518). The singer glorifies his calling and his audience by comparing his performance to that of a great hero before the fabulous Phaeacians, but perhaps there is also the meaning that action and the song of action are in a way one – he who does the deeds is creating the song and hearing its resonance. Again the simile is simple and striking, one of many in the *Odyssey* drawn from skilled trades: the similes which accompany the action of blinding the Cyclops are the most remarkable instance (9.383–94).

As often at intense moments, the pace of action quickens, and the intervention of Zeus takes less than one whole line to narrate. The adjective 'naked' of the arrow comes, as so often in the Homeric poems, by itself at the beginning of a line, as for instance when Athena says to Zeus 'My heart is burning for the prudent Odysseus, *luckless one*, who is suffering far from home' (1.47–8): as often, it is a heavy and pregnant epithet. One arrow is stripped for action, as in a moment Odysseus 'stripped off his rags' (22.1) in a gesture which flung off his old beggarly identity: the same word is used – *gumnos*, the naked arrow – *gumnōthē,* he stripped. The verb used of the Suitors 'sampling' the arrows – *peirēsesthai* – was used twenty lines earlier of Odysseus 'trying' the bow, *peirōmenos*: that introduces a grim humour – the Suitors will 'try' it in a very different sense. The unruffled superiority which Odysseus expresses in taking his time over checking his bow, then stringing it without apparent exertion, is continued as he shoots sitting down and addresses Telemachus with darkly playful irony. The Suitors have long feasted with music: now for a feast of death, and then for a real celebration. There will in fact be music and dancing when the Suitors are dead, a ruse of Odysseus to conceal their killing (23.143ff). All the passages in the poem which bear on hospitality and its abuses, and on meals and gruesome scenes during meals – the killing of Agamemnon, the cannibalism of the Cyclops — are to be felt as active behind the last grisly scene which now commences.

12. The epic style: technique and variety

Some procedures which are natural to Homeric style are worth a word of comment. In general expression it is paratactic: that is, it proceeds by adding separate clauses and sentences rather than by such 'subordinate' connections as 'although' or 'after'. Thus Odysseus answers Eurymachus' challenge that he is a work-shy idler:

Eurymachus, I wish there could be a contest in work between us — in the spring time, when days are long — in the hay, I would have a curved sickle, and you would have the same, that we might try our hand at work — fasting right up to the sunset, and hay were there in plenty: or if there were oxen to drive, those which are the best, tawny and big, both fed full on hay, oxen of the same age and power — their strength is not slight — and there were a day's measure of land, and the tilth were yielding to the plough: then you would see me, if I would drive a straight furrow. (18.366–75)

It is noticeable how many independent elements with verbs there are in this passage, which in English, or in later Greek, would be broken up into subordinate clauses.

We can observe also a tendency to repeat an important word, lingering on it. This is essentially, like parataxis, a device of unsophisticated speech, though Homer's use of it may be far from naive. In a simple form we find things like the description of Hermes arriving on Calypso's island. Her cave was worth seeing:

There even an immortal who came by would *marvel* at the sight and delight his mind. There stood the Messenger, Argus-slayer, and *marvelled*; and when he *had marvelled* at it all in his heart. . .(5.74–6)

There is a greater difference in the verb forms in Greek than in English — *thēēsaito*, *thēeito*, *thēēsato* — but the repetition is enjoyed for its own sake. A spectacular instance comes in Book Nineteen. Odysseus, disguised, is talking to Penelope about her husband, whom he claims to have entertained in Crete, a false tale but like the truth:

And as she listened her tears flowed and her flesh *melted* [or 'wasted', but we need this verb here]: as snow *melts* on the high hills, snow which the east wind *melts away* when the west wind has showered it down, and as it *melts* the rivers are brimmed full with it: even so did her fair cheeks *melt* as she shed tears, weeping for the husband who was sitting beside her.   (19.204–9)

Forms of the verb *tēko* appear no less than five times in five lines, and since the passage is a simile, a decorative poetical device of a sophisticated kind, the explanation is clearly not simple incapacity to think of another word. The resemblance between pining Penelope and melting snow is hammered home by this device of loving repetition.

Extended similes are one of the glories of the Homeric epic. To say 'he came like an eagle' or 'he raged like a bull' is common to many poetic traditions: peculiar to Homer is the elaborate comparison, which may run to eight or ten lines. They are notably commoner in the *Iliad*, where they multiply particularly in the scenes of killing in battle; not because the poet thinks such scenes are boring and wants to liven them up, but from a desire to make these terrible scenes as vivid as possible to the mind of the audience. The *Odyssey* contains fewer passages of intense writing than the *Iliad*, but moments such as the blinding of the Cyclops or the stringing of the bow are underlined and made vivid by full-dress comparisons. Most of the similes in the *Iliad* are drawn from the fierce terrors of nature – storms, forest-fires, lions. When the *Odyssey* uses such material, which is seldom, a change can be seen. In the *Iliad* a lion attacks the cattle in the byre, 'and his haughty spirit drives him on': that simile is applied to a great Trojan hero attacking the Greek lines (*Iliad* 12.299–308). In the *Odyssey* Odysseus, shipwrecked, naked, hungry, caked in brine, has to approach the princess Nausicaa and her maids to beg for help: 'He went on like a lion of the mountains, trusting in his strength, which goes through rain and wind . . . his belly drives him on' (6.130–4). The change from 'his haughty spirit' to 'his belly' is a significant one, conveying something of the different atmosphere of the two poems. Odysseus is always talking about his belly and its imperious

demands (15.344, 17.286, 17.473, 18.53, 18.380): *that* is the
sort of lion which he would resemble, hungry and bedraggled.

Others, as we saw in section 11, relate to trades. The red-
hot spit rotating in the eye of the Cyclops is like a drill
rotating to bore a plank; the sizzling of the eye is like that
when a newly forged axe is dipped by the blacksmith into
cold water (9.384–4). The bizarre episode is made vividly
realisable by these familiar touches. We find an extraordinarily suggestive comparison when Odysseus, having asked
Demodocus for a song about the Trojan Horse, weeps bitterly
as he hears it,

As a woman weeps, throwing herself on her dear husband, who has
fallen in defence of his city and people, trying to ward off enslave-
ment from town and children: she, seeing him gasping and dying,
flings herself on him with shrill lament; but they come behind her,
beating her back and shoulders with their spears, and take her into
slavery, to undergo labour and misery; her cheeks are ravaged by
most pitiful woe: even so did Odysseus shed a pitiful tear beneath
his brows.   (8.523–31)

Odysseus, city-sacker, has done his share of this sort of thing
in his time. Only seventy lines later in the unfolding of the
poem, but years earlier in time, he treated the Cicones just so:

There I sacked the city and slew the men, and from the city we took
their wives and all their property and divided it up, so that no one
should be deprived of his fair share.   (9.40–2)

Now he finds himself alone and dependent, all the booty lost
long ago: the story which was his pride is now too tragic to
listen to, as through the medium of song he learns to sym-
pathise with suffering, to feel it as his own. Victorious hero
and helpless victim, apparently so far apart, are brought close
together in the shared experience of tears, and it is their
likeness, not their difference, which the poet sees.

That remarkable simile recalls two others, in which again
there is discernible something like the reversal involved in
comparing the conquering hero to a conquered woman.
Odysseus, shipwrecked and swimming for his life, is finally
lifted by a wave and able to spy land in the distance. The sight
is as welcome to him as signs of recovery in a long sick father

are to his anxious children (5.394–8). Much later, when Penelope finally recognises her husband,

As when land appears, a welcome sight to men swimming, whose well-made ship Poseidon has wrecked in the open sea, driving it with wind and breaking wave: few escape from the grey sea to land, with much brine caked on their skin; welcome is the land as they come ashore, surviving their sufferings: even so to her was her husband welcome as she gazed at him.   (23.233–9)

The comparison inescapably recalls the actual experience of Odysseus. What Penelope has undergone, different as it seemed, has been like his masculine adventures, and at the moment of reunion their experience seems to form a unity. That is underlined by the parallel with the domestic simile – sick father, anxious children – which was appropriate to Odysseus at a moment of heroic effort and danger.

   These are sophisticated effects, running in a way counter to the straightforwardness of the normal epic. That does not mean that they are merely the fantasy of the modern reader. Let us compare another unusual moment, of a rather different sort. In Book Nineteen Penelope and the disguised Odysseus hold a long confidential conversation. In the course of it Penelope weeps with extraordinary abandon: the passage, with its simile of the melting snow – we seem to see the emotional ice melting – was quoted earlier in this chapter. She is reminded of Odysseus as never before, yet still she refuses to believe that he is alive (19.560–81), and at the end of the book they separate for the night: I, says Penelope, in my bed of constant tears, you somewhere in the house (19.584–9). That separation, their last and deftly underlined by the poet, is developed in Book Twenty. Penelope dreams that her husband is sleeping beside her, a dream so vivid that she took it for reality; when she wakes she speaks of it with tears, and Odysseus hears her voice as he lies in his own improvised bed, 'and it seemed to him in his heart that she, already recognising him, was standing beside his head' (19.83–94). We must feel here that husband and wife, after their talk, are each strongly aware of the proximity of the other, in ways for which they cannot account. The *Odyssey* is the ultimate ancestor of the Greek novels and so of the European novel, and here we feel a psychological density which recalls the novel rather than the epic: nothing, in a sense, 'happens', but feelings are developed for their own sake.

Nothing is more characteristic of Homer than the great amount of direct speech in the poems. Including Odysseus' narration of his own adventures, more than half the *Odyssey* is in direct speech. Like the narrative, speeches can vary greatly in tone and pace. Time stands still during the long stories told by Nestor and Menelaus, or during the false tales with which Odysseus amuses people on Ithaca ('I gazed at him as at a bard', says Eumaeus). Other dialogues can be positively laconic. For instance, two competing messengers come to tell Penelope of her son's return: one blurts it out in a single line, 'Your son is home, my queen' (16.337). Later in that book we find guarded and curt speech. 'Let's tell *them* to come back', says Eurymachus, meaning their ambush party: no point in staying on now. But another Suitor has seen the ambush ship returning, and he says 'Let us not send a message: they are here. Either a god told them, or they saw the ship going past and could not catch it.' 'How the gods have got him out of trouble!' says Antinous bitterly (16.346–64). All these utterances are both short and also deliberately unrevealing. 'Them', 'they', 'him', 'the ship', are all things which must not be named out loud. Book Seventeen contains other conversations like this, which show that the formal manner ('the black ship of god-like Telemachus') is not the only one at the disposal of the *Odyssey*.

Indirect speech is not favoured by the poet. The seven lines in which Demodocus' song about Troy is reported (8.514–20) are exceptional, caused by the poet's reluctance to go into details when what interests him is only the effect on Odysseus. The thirty-line narration of Odysseus' adventures at 23.310–41 is not in the Homeric style, and that is one reason for regarding the very end of the poem as not authentic (see section 15). On the whole narrators are omniscient, telling us things which they could only have found out later,

if at all, as if they were aware of them at the time. For instance Eumaeus, in the touching and lively story he tells of his
being kidnapped by his nurse and a band of pirates when he
was little — 'a cunning little fellow, just trotting out of doors
with me', the nurse calls him (15.451) — reports for us all the
details of the woman's assignation and conversation with the
pirates (15.421ff), and when Odysseus goes up to a look-out
he sees, not just smoke, but 'smoke from the house of Circe'
(10.150). But there are moments when awareness is shown of
this point. Hermes tells Calypso that she must let Odysseus
go. She is forced to comply, but she tells Odysseus only that
'My mind is righteous, and my heart in my breast is not of
iron: no, it is merciful' (5.190 – 1). Naturally Odysseus is
astonished, and he never does find out why she did it: he tells
the Phaeacians it was 'At a summons from Zeus, or else her
own mind changed' (7.263). Calypso, very humanly, wants
the credit for her enforced action. More remarkably, in Book
Twelve Odysseus tells us of a conversation on Olympus between Zeus and the Sun-god. At the end of it he adds, 'This
I heard from Calypso, and she said she heard it from Hermes
the messenger' (12.389–90). This surprising touch shows a
sudden twinge of conscience on the poet's part: how *did*
Odysseus know all this? Perhaps it was mentioned in the conversation quoted in Book Five.

   Special to the *Odyssey* is the poet's art of transitions. A certain pleasure in complexity is shown in the conception of
beginning the poem with Odysseus and Telemachus in different places, then putting them through separate adventures
before uniting them. It involves turning from one place and
theme to another. Athena sets the stage, for instance, when
she tells Odysseus that he is to stay in Eumaeus' hut and ask
him questions, while she goes to Sparta to set Telemachus on
his homeward journey (13.411–15). We see Odysseus settle
down for the night, and as he sleeps Athena goes off to
Telemachus, fast asleep in Sparta (14.523–15.45). That is an
elegant transition, smoothed by the shared idea of sleep.
Almost as smooth is that when Odysseus wakes to meet
Nausicaa. One girl throws the ball into the river, they all cry

out, and Odysseus wakes (6.117). Towards the end of Book
Four events pass from Sparta to the Suitors in Ithaca (4.624),
then to Penelope (4.675), then back to the Suitors (4.768), to
Penelope (4.787), and to the Suitors laying their ambush far
away (4.842). It seems natural to think that this deft handling
of several strands was a speciality of the poet of the *Odyssey*,
and that he enjoyed such displays of virtuosity, which suggests a certain self-consciousness on his part.

A last aspect of the *Odyssey* which strikes every reader is
its irony; that, too, is a self-conscious device. The plot involves a hero whose identity is unknown to many of the
people among whom he moves: that was natural once he has
returned incognito to Ithaca, but the scene among the Phaeacians need not have been developed in the same way, with
Odysseus concealing his identity for hundreds of lines and
only giving hints by his tears at Demodocus' Trojan songs,
had not the poet positively enjoyed such effects.

They also are prominent in the first four books. Thus when
Telemachus, encouraged by Athena in her disguise as Mentes,
tells the Suitors to get out of his house, Antinous replies,
'Telemachus, the gods themselves must be teaching you to
speak up so boldly' (1.384). That is, as we know, truer than
he thinks. At Pylos, Telemachus is seized with shyness about
addressing the aged Nestor. Athena, again disguised, says to
him, 'Telemachus, some things you will think of yourself,
and others a god will put into your thoughts' (3.26). She
means herself. In Pylos the newcomers are invited to join in
a ceremony of prayers to Poseidon. Athena knows, and we
know, that it really is Poseidon who is the obstacle to
Odysseus' return, but to the other characters this special
significance is unknown. So she prays: '"Hear us, Poseidon
Earth-shaker, and do not grudge us the fulfilment of these
our prayers . . ."' So she prayed, and she fulfilled it all
herself' (3.55–62). We share her pleasure, and that of the
poet, at seeing a meaning behind the surface of events.

When Odysseus is moving unrecognised in his own house,
such effects take on a deeper meaning. Even the Suitors are
aware, as they anxiously tell Antinous, that gods move

disguised among men, in the shape of strangers, testing men for violence and good behaviour (18.481 – 7): suppose this beggar is a god? The poet derives special ironic effects from Odysseus' incognito, many things being said by him or in his presence which gain added meaning from knowledge of his identity. That goes furthest when Penelope is made to say to Eurycleia, 'Come, wash the feet of your master's contemporary' (19.358). The effect is much less unnatural in the Greek, and cannot be fully conveyed in English without overemphasis. In the context of recognition, the hint has a poignant quality. Odysseus allows himself several heavily ironical utterances, through which his true self peeps out. 'Be generous', he says to Antinous: 'I too was rich once and lived in a fine house' (17.419). Later he says that no labour will tire him, he will hold up the torches for the Suitors, 'Even if they decide to stay till morning they will not beat me: I am muchenduring' (18.319). We hear the allusion, lost on the Suitors, to his regular epithet, 'much-enduring Odysseus'; and 'they will not beat me' also looks forward, for us but not for them, to his battle with them. In the same vein is Penelope's first notice of the mysterious beggar. Perhaps he has seen or heard of Odysseus, 'for he is like a man of many travels' (17.50). Greek does not express 'a', and the line looks as if it could mean 'He is like the great traveller.' A last instance: when the bow is produced, the first of the Suitors to try and fail to draw it says

My friends, I cannot draw it: let someone else take it. Many noblemen will this bow deprive of life and breath, since it is better to die than to live on and fail in our purpose. (21.152–4)

That speech, evidently designed for the sake of its ironic opening, is truer than the speaker knows.

Odysseus was compared to a god, judging men among whom he moves in secret. That is indeed his role: Athena urges him to try all the Suitors and see which of them are lawless and which are better (17.363), and he also tests his servants for their loyalty (21.209–11), while his destruction of the Suitors is repeatedly said to be the work of outraged heaven.

He is indeed the first to say so himself (22.413–16), and both
Penelope and Laertes agree (23.63–6, 24.360). It is in harmony with this that his victory is foreshadowed by dreams
and omens. Some of these have the same ironic character,
bringing out again the poet's delight in irony. Thus when
Odysseus holds up the lights for the Suitors, one of them
makes a joke: 'It's by the will of God that this man has come
to Odysseus' house – his bald head reflects the light so
well' (18.351–5). And more explicitly, when Odysseus has
knocked out the beggar Irus, Antinous is delighted and says
'May Zeus grant you whatever you most want, for disposing
of that greedy wretch.' And, says the poet, 'Odysseus was
pleased by the omen' (18.112–17), for Antinous was un-
consciously praying for his own death.

13. The *Odyssey* and the *Iliad*

The poet of the *Iliad* created a poem of a very special sort.
In the first place it is extremely long. Secondly, he set out to
produce something which would represent the whole of the
Trojan War, while actually narrating only a small and apparently not very important set of incidents in it. At the
beginning of the *Iliad* the Achaeans have already been at Troy
for ten years; at the end of the poem the city is still standing,
and even Achilles, the doomed hero, is still alive. Yet with
great skill both the start of the war (in Book Three) and the
death of Achilles and the fall of Troy (in Books Eighteen,
Twenty-Two, and Twenty-Four) have been included, by indirect means, within the poem.

That combination of intense focus and broad comprehen-
siveness is an extraordinary one. A few weeks out of ten
years, and the anger of Achilles and its consequences, are illuminated in detail and at length, and they give an interpretation of the whole enormous story. The poet of the *Odyssey*
was familiar with the *Iliad*. That he is composing a little later
is independently suggested by such things as the rather different representation of the gods (see section 19), the presence
everywhere of Phoenician sailors, a few linguistic details

which suggest a slightly later stage in the tradition. It is also pretty clear that the *Iliad* exercised much influence over the *Odyssey*.

First and most important is the whole conception of the poem. The return home of Odysseus was not, before the *Odyssey*, one of the supreme points of the Trojan saga. The beginning of the war, with the abduction by Paris of Helen, and the end of the war, with the Trojan Horse, were more obvious peaks. Among the return stories, that which stood out was the grim tale of the home-coming of Agamemnon. The Odysseus story, by contrast, had an ultimately happy ending, and it took place not, like that of Agamemnon, in a great city in the heart of Greece, but on a remote Western island. The poet of the *Odyssey* has set himself the task of making that story rival in length the great epic of Achilles, and also draw in and include all the stories which came after the end of the *Iliad*: the fall of Troy and the various home-comings (*nostoi*) of the victorious Achaeans.

Thus the *Odyssey* was bound to become very long and also to be focused on one man. Achilles in the *Iliad* withdraws from the stage — though constantly and deftly kept in our thoughts — for much of the poem: Odysseus is off stage for the first four books of the *Odyssey*, but everything which happens relates to him and reminds us of him. The destiny of Achilles goes on after the end of the *Iliad*, and we are told that his death in battle is now at hand: the destiny of Odysseus goes on after the end of the *Odyssey* (11.119–37). He must go on another journey, to a land so far from the sea that he is asked whether the oar he carries on his shoulder is a winnowing-fan. Then he can make peace at last with the angry Poseidon, and grow old in prosperity at home, awaiting a gentle death in peace. That surely shows both an echo of the *Iliad* and the fate of Achilles, and also a conscious reversal of its atmosphere: not a violent death, soon, at the gates of Troy, but a gentle death, far ahead, at home.

The events of the *Iliad* took place in the tenth year of the war. That is a point which produces certain difficulties for the poet: the heroes, especially Achilles, seem younger than that lapse of time must make them (who can imagine an Achilles aged thirty?), and the problems of feeding and providing for an army for so long are, if we think about them, formidable. The *Odyssey* sets its story in the tenth year after the war. That produces certain difficulties, too: Odysseus has to be delayed somewhere for a really long time, and Penelope, twenty years after her husband sailed away leaving her with a young child (11.447–9), is a little mature to be quite as irresistible as her importunate Suitors find her. It is natural to think that the *Odyssey* is here echoing, or rivalling, the *Iliad*: these events, too, took ten years to unfold.

By the time Odysseus makes his way back to Ithaca, all the other heroes have long been either at home or dead – or, like Agamemnon, both. Ten years separate the time of the action from the fall of Troy. The *Odyssey* shows itself anxious to fill in that gap, to tell what happened at Troy, and to show us the great people of the *Iliad* and to tell us their stories. We hear of the death and funeral of Achilles (24.34–97). The Wooden Horse is the subject of a song by Demodocus which Odysseus weeps to hear (8.499–520). Menelaus describes the ambiguous conduct of Helen when the Horse was drawn into Troy (4.266–89), and Odysseus himself tells Achilles' ghost of being inside the Horse, the anxieties of the heroes, and the heroic conduct of Achilles' son (11.523–37). After the sack of Troy, summarily described at 8.514–20, the Achaeans did not behave well. Their departure from Troy was drunken and chaotic, as Nestor sadly tells Telemachus (3.130ff), and their old ally Athena was bitterly angry with them:

When we had sacked the tall city of Priam, then did the mind of Zeus devise a disastrous return for the Argives, since not all of them had been prudent or righteous: therefore they suffered an evil fate, many of them, in consequence of the grim wrath of the grey-eyed daughter of that mighty sire.   (3.130–5)

What had they done to enrage their patron goddess? The poet knows, and assumes that we know, the story: the lesser Ajax, son of Oileus, a second-rank hero, raped the Trojan princess Cassandra, dragging her away from Athena's altar. The failure of the other Achaeans to punish this horrid act involved them all in his guilt. Ajax himself came to a terrible end, wrecked on his way home and then killed by Poseidon, a detail which comes not in the speech of Nestor but in that of Menelaus (4.499–510) – the stories are carefully distributed through the poem – and Athena 'imposed a cruel return' on the Achaeans generally (1.325–6).

The story of Agamemnon, as we saw in section 6, is touched on repeatedly: we hear different details and allusions, not all perfectly reconcilable, from Nestor, from Menelaus, and twice from Agamemnon himself (3.254ff, 4.512ff, 11.405ff, 24.192ff). Not only is it a fascinating tale and the end of a great hero: it also provides an explicit parallel to the story of Odysseus. 'Be warned by what happened to me', says Agamemnon to Odysseus, 'and don't put too much trust in your wife – yet you at least are safe from death at your wife's hands: she is too sensible and well balanced, Icarius' daughter, the prudent Penelope' (11.441–6). In the first book, Athena has not been talking long to Telemachus before she says to him that he must turn his mind to killing the Suitors. He is too old now to go on being helpless, and Orestes is a shining example:

Do you not hear how much glory noble Orestes has won everywhere, since he killed his father's murderer, crafty Aegisthus? You too, my friend since I see you so tall and well made, you must be valiant, that those who come after may glorify you.   (1.298–302)

The same note is struck again in Pylos, when Nestor says 'You have heard of the death and avenging of Agamemnon – Such a good thing it is when a dead man leaves a son: Orestes has slain his father's murderer. You should be valiant, too' (3.193–200, compressed; some of the same lines recur here). If Penelope had been like Agamemnon's wife Clytemnestra, then he might have faced a crueller homecoming – and Telemachus might have had to avenge him. No wonder he sometimes thinks grim thoughts about his mother (1.215–20, cf. 15.14–23).

Meditation on the doom of Agamemnon suggested to the poet, or to his audience, an obvious question: Why did his brother Menelaus, for whose sake after all he had fought the

Trojan War, do nothing to avenge him? Telemachus puts this question to Nestor: Where was Menelaus? Was he out of the country? (3.247–52). Nestor tells him that unfortunately Menelaus was blown off course and fetched up in Egypt (3.294ff); and so he got home too late, and Orestes had already killed Aegisthus – Menelaus arrived on the very last day of the funeral, in fact. This suggested a further development: the wanderings of Menelaus, as that hero himself describes them, are given by the poet a striking parallelism to those of Odysseus (see section 10).

The last thing which the *Odyssey* poet got from the Agamemnon story was from reflection on the role of Orestes. The story of the hero who must come home in the nick of time to save his wife and kingdom is very common in many literatures, and it is exceptional for him to have a son to help him. Giving an important role to Telemachus enabled the poem to be enlarged both in bulk and in scope, and to show us the maturing of the young hero. Its importance for the *Odyssey* is incalculable. And it arose, in all likelihood, from brooding on the great hero of the *Iliad* and his connection with Odysseus.

Nestor, Menelaus, and of course Helen, the people whom Telemachus meets on his journey, are great figures of the *Iliad*, whom those who had listened to the song of their exploits in war were naturally delighted to see again at home in peace. We even meet Achilles among the dead: his ideas on life and death have changed since the *Iliad*. In section 19 we shall discuss the new heroism of the *Odyssey*, and the striking contrast which it presents, in some ways, with the older epic. It will be appropriate here to give a couple of specific examples of Iliadic influence.

The opening of the *Odyssey* – 'Sing me the man, O Muse, who . . .' is, I think, meant to recall that of the *Iliad*: 'Tell me of the wrath, goddess, which . . .' In the Greek the first word is 'Man –', an effect impossible to recapture in English: it evokes the Iliadic first word 'Wrath –'. As has often been said, the first word of each of the two poems states the theme of the whole. Each prologue goes on to expound the divine purpose in all this: in the *Iliad*, 'the will of Zeus was fulfilled' (*Iliad* 1.5); in the *Odyssey*, the offence against the Sun, who doomed Odysseus' companions for their sin (*Odyssey* 1.7–9). Athena can start the ball rolling for Odysseus' return because Poseidon is away from Olympus, among the Ethiopians (1.22–4): that exploits a motif from later in the *Iliad*, Book One, where all the gods have gone off to feast with the Ethiopians. The derivative nature of the *Odyssey* passage is shown by the fact that it goes on 'the Ethiopians, who dwell in two groups, most remote of men: some where the sun will set, some where he will rise' (1.23–4). Ethiopians, 'Burnt-faces', live in the places where the Sun comes closest: that is, presumably, where he rises and sets. But the learned, or ingenious, addition only confuses: to which lot of Ethiopians has Poseidon gone? More examples could be given, but the role of Telemachus, the absence from the scene of Odysseus, and the wording of the prologue, show how great was the influence of the *Iliad* on the *Odyssey*.

We shall see in section 19 how the Odyssean conception of heroism − crafty, long-suffering, biding its time − contrasts with the passionate and dashing heroism of Achilles, and how in at least one place the *Odyssey* gives its explicit answer to the *Iliad*. We can end this section with a couple of examples of the contrast in atmosphere and ethos between the two poems. The extent to which the *Odyssey* is presenting us consciously with variants on the *Iliad* will forever be open to question; the comparisons are in any case revealing, and my own view is that the later poem is indeed consciously exploiting the earlier.

In the first book of the *Iliad* Achilles has a violent quarrel with Agamemnon. Deciding against his original impulse to strike his opponent dead on the spot, he announces in a vehement speech that he will withdraw from the fighting. He swears an oath

'By this sceptre, which will never grow leaves and twigs, since it has been cut on the hills, nor will it live on, for the bronze has lopped off its leaves and bark; now the Achaeans carry it in their hands when they administer justice, the precedents that come from Zeus;

that shall be my mighty oath: longing for Achilles shall come on the sons of the Achaeans, every one of them, when they fall dying in multitudes at the hands of man-slaying Hector . . .' So spoke Achilles, and he flung to the ground the sceptre with its studs of gold.   (*Iliad* 1.234–46)

That is a powerful speech and a gesture to match. Judges hold that sceptre; it is held by a speaker at an assembly to show that he 'has the floor'. Achilles first builds up its significance with a long account, then throws it down as a symbol of rejection of the most hallowed order of society.

In the *Odyssey* Telemachus calls an assembly, the first for twenty years, and holding a sceptre (2.37) he makes a long speech denouncing the Suitors and begging for the support of the people. At the end of it, 'He threw down the sceptre, bursting into tears: pity seized the whole gathering' (2.80–1). The same gesture, but what a contrast! Not the terrible hero threatening vengeance and breaking with his society, but a helpless young man, unable to go on, throwing down the sceptre in despair.

Later in the first book of the *Iliad* Achilles sits by himself on the shore, in tears, gazing over the boundless sea, until his mother the sea-nymph comes in response to his distress and promises to invoke Zeus for him against Agamemnon. The scene expresses his self-imposed isolation from other men, his passionate and solitary nature, and also his privileged access to the gods. In the fifth book of the *Odyssey* our first sight of Odysseus, long awaited, recalls that scene. Calypso, instructed to release him, goes to find him:

She found him sitting on the shore; his eyes were never dry of tears, and his sweet life was dripping away as he mourned for his home . . . Every day, sitting among the rocks on the shore, he would gaze over the barren sea shedding tears.   (5.151–8)

Again similarity, and again difference. Achilles by his presence on the shore called up his loving and powerful mother; Odysseus came day after day, weeping hopelessly, with no prospect that anything would come of it. Each Odyssean scene is touching, melancholy, rather than passionate. It can surely not be an accident that scenes so near the beginning of the *Iliad* seem to have helped suggest them, and by contrast help us to appreciate them.

14. Myth and folklore

Greek myth is dominated by the careers of heroes, great figures who were closer to the gods than we are, but who none the less were men and died. Most of the mythologies of the world are very different, dominated by gods, talking animals, and monsters (things not unknown, of course, in Greek myth). Heroes contend with other heroes, in a world run by gods and goddesses who are like men and women on a larger scale, stronger, handsomer, and freed from old age and death. Monster-slaying heroes like Heracles and Perseus are a small and rather separate category: gods do not, as for instance in Egypt, have animal forms.

A mythology of this sort is a special creation, the work of the poets, and there are many traces to be found of other, less anthropomorphic ideas, fears and fantasies. What interests us here is the literary aspect of all this. The *Iliad* is austere in excluding from the world magic, spooks, monsters, and the uncanny, and concentrating the essence of heroism in the armed man facing death at the hands of a heroic enemy. Even the greatest hero, Achilles, must die, and his death is a real one — no posthumous blessedness, of the sort imagined for him by most later Greeks. That is all essential for the tragic aspect of the poem. Horrid myths like Iphigenia being sacrificed by her own father are ignored, too, and we hear very little of the great gods Demeter and Dionysus, gods of ecstasy and of initiation and privilege after death.

The *Odyssey*, influenced as it is by the *Iliad*, has on the whole the same conception. Great Achilles speaks with bitterness of the miserable lot of the dead, and Odysseus must die; and warlike heroism is admired and extolled. Menelaus, it is true, tells us that he is explicitly exempted from death and marked out for the Elysian Fields, but that is only his account of the matter (4.561 – 9), and the poet never himself gives anyone such a destiny. As for warfare, Odysseus is city-sacker, and that is glorious; but we saw in section 12 a simile which seemed to cast doubt on it, and other passages do so more explicitly. The good Eumaeus says to Odysseus that the gods do not love violence but righteousness, and that even those who are aggressive and hostile, who go raiding and come back with ships full of loot, even they feel great dread afterwards (14.83–8). That speech seems to condemn Odysseus himself. Penelope tells him that

He who is hard and has hard ways, on him all men call down disaster in his life, and after his death all curse him; but he who is righteous and has righteous ways, his fame is broadcast everywhere, and many are those who praise him.   (19.329–34)

The old myth doubtless told of Odysseus alone shooting down all the Suitors with his great bow, but the *Odyssey* is influenced by the chivalrous ideas of classical Greece, which regarded the bow and long-distance combat as unmanly and valued hand-to-hand combat with the spear. That must be why Odysseus, originally so committed an archer that he named his son Telemachus ('fighter at a distance'), must run out of arrows, arm in the middle of the battle, and finish off the Suitors spear in hand.

There is a constant source of difficulty, in fact, in combining the hero of the Wanderings, who meets witches and ogres, with the hero who fought at Troy, lived in a definite historical setting, and had to come to terms with political and economic problems. As the leader of a contingent at Troy, Odysseus has twelve ships full of men. In the Wanderings they are an embarrassment to him. Only in the attack on the Cicones, the first exploit and the most Iliadic, have they a role to play. In the adventure with the Cyclops all ships but one must be left somewhere else ('You stay here, the rest of my loyal men, and I will go with my own ship and my own companions' (9.172–3)), and really it is only the crew of one ship which can open the bag of the winds which he is given by Aeolus. The others are removed by the transparent device of making all moor within the Laestrygonian harbour except Odysseus, who moors outside (10.91–6). That enables all the others to be destroyed and Odysseus to meet Circe,

Scylla and Charybdis, and the Underworld, with a single ship.

We can see that an order has been imposed on these adventures, which in origin are separate. First a regular heroic fleet of a dozen ships, capable of exploits, meeting first with reasonably innocuous adventures and finally with unmanageable disaster; then the pattern is repeated with the single ship; and finally Odysseus, having been rescued by Calypso, is reduced to the lowest point on the human scale. No longer the admiral of a fleet nor even the captain of a ship, he loses even his hand-made boat and the clothes the nymph gave him: naked, hungry, dishevelled, he can keep himself alive only by heaping up a pile of leaves and sleeping inside it. Then his ascent begins, as he is progressively bathed, fed, clothed, welcomed, and accepted by the Phaeacians, even before he reveals his name, as an impressive person worthy to be given rich presents and sent on his way as a hero.

And the disasters which destroy his men are presented, as far as possible, as being their own fault. At the beginning of the poem we hear that Odysseus was anxious to secure safe homecoming for his men but could not save them: 'By their own reckless folly were they destroyed, for devouring the cattle of the Sun' (1.7–8). The basic shape of the story demands that the hero return home alone, not with twelve ships at his back. When that story became attached to the leader of a contingent, the story-shape doomed his men. The poet is anxiously aware that it does not look well when the king is the sole survivor, and the kinsmen of the Suitors make the point explicitly (24.426–8). It was their own sin, the poet insists, which destroyed his men. There has to be some sleight of hand in this, as in fact it is only the last ship which the anger of the Sun destroys − the rest were already smashed and the men devoured by the Laestrygonians, on the occasion when Odysseus cannily moored his ship separately from theirs. The men are indeed foolish creatures, throwing away their return by opening Aeolus' bag (but might not Odysseus have departed from his normal policy of mistrust by telling them what was in it?), but when the insubordinate officer Eurylochus tries to stir up a mutiny, saying that it was

Odysseus who got their other companions killed (10.431–7)
– 'It was through this man's reckless folly that they were
destroyed', an echo of 1.7, quoted above – he has some
justice on his side. It was Odysseus who took the party into
the Cyclops' cave, out of curiosity and acquisitiveness. His
men implored him not to stay and meet the monster, and
again not to reveal his name after his escape – an act which
enables the Cyclops to curse him effectively (9.224–30,
491ff).

In that last case Odysseus tells us 'They did not prevail on
my great-hearted spirit', and so he insisted on uttering the
triumphant boast of a hero, like the boast of a victor in an
Iliadic duel over the body of his dead opponent. It is an
example of something which recurs: Odysseus strives to be a
proper hero in situations which make it impossible. Here are
two examples. When he comes face to face with the monstrous
figure of the Cyclops and is asked who he is and what he is
doing, 'Our hearts were broken within us in fear of his deep
voice and vast size. But still I answered him –' and it begins
as a brave speech: 'We are the Achaeans, we took Troy, we
are the people of Agamemnon, the most glorious man on
earth. But now we come to you as suppliants, if you will give
us a gift of hospitality. Respect the gods: Zeus avenges
wrongs to suppliants and guests' (9.250–71). We hear the
touching change of tone: we are great heroes – don't kill us!
For what use is it to be a hero when faced by a cannibal ogre?
Again, when Circe tells him how Scylla will take some of his
men, he asks whether he cannot avenge himself on her. 'Rash
man', Circe replies, 'will you still be thinking of fighting?
Will you not bow even to gods? Scylla is not mortal but a
deathless monster, not to be fought with. There is no defence,
to flee is best' (12.111–20). But when Odysseus actually
comes to it, 'then I forgot the hard instructions of Circe, who
told me not to put on my armour', and he arms with helmet
and two spears: but to no avail, Scylla still seizes six of his
men and carries them off: 'There outside her lair she
devoured them as they shrieked, holding out their arms to me
in their agony. That was the most pathetic sight I ever saw'

(12.226–58). The combination of two kinds of story and two kinds of heroism, the Achillean fighter and the folk-tale hero who must rely on his wits, produces effects of curiously touching pathos.

15. Some problems

In section 6 we saw that there are passages in the Odyssey which seem to go with a different version of events: the hero identifying himself to his wife and planning the destruction of the Suitors in complicity with her. In section 18 we shall discuss the difficulties raised by the constitutional position on Ithaca, the questions of the succession to Odysseus and the aspirations of the Suitors: does Penelope's husband become king? In both cases it emerges that there is no simple explanation. The story of Odysseus could be sung in different ways, even by the poet of the *Odyssey* himself, and there was a tendency for these ways to co-exist in the full-length treatment of the great epic.

We can now turn to three other apparent difficulties, one near the beginning of the poem and two near the end. The first is superficially puzzling but not really difficult. At the beginning of Book One there is a discussion among the gods of the position of Odysseus. Athena says to Zeus that, if the blessed gods agree that Odysseus should return home,

Then let us send Hermes the Messenger, Argus-slayer, to the Ogygian isle, to tell the nymph, Calypso of the lovely locks, our true purpose, the return of long-suffering Odysseus, so that he may go; and I will go to Ithaca to stir up his son and put spirit in his heart.

(1.81 – 9)

These two things happen, as usual in Homer, in the reverse order, Athena coming down to Telemachus forthwith, and Hermes going to Calypso in Book Five. But before he goes, another scene of council is described on Olympus. Athena opens it with a speech about Odysseus' plight, and then Zeus addresses Hermes and tells him to go to Calypso.

What is the relation of these two councils? According to a count of time, a week has elapsed since Athena went to

Ithaca, and Hermes has done nothing. This is in fact an example of a general rule of Homeric style, that events are presented in an unbroken stream of successive time: the narrator does not go back and forward in time, as his characters can do in their speeches. While he is describing the coming of Athena and its consequence in the trip of Telemachus, Hermes and Odysseus cannot move. When they do move, it is presented as in chronological succession to Athena's journey; and the divine council which despatches Hermes in Book Five is, in a sense, a purely stylistic doublet of the divine council in Book One. The question why nothing has happened for a week about the first decision is one which cannot be pressed.

It follows from what we have just said that Telemachus, having reached Sparta, will have to stay there until we have finished with Odysseus' strand of events and can go back to him. If the days are counted, he stays at Sparta for a long time: Odysseus sails his boat, after all, for eighteen days (5.279). It is not to the point to invent motives for this long stay, by pointing for instance to Athena's statement to Odysseus that she will get Telemachus moving: 'I shall go to Sparta of the fair women to call Telemachus, who has gone off to Lacedaemon of the fine dancing grounds in search of tidings of you' (13.412–15), and inferring that Telemachus is having such a good time dancing with pretty girls in Sparta, home of Helen, that he does not want to leave. It is Homeric narration which makes it impossible for him to go earlier.

Two other subjects can be discussed here. One is the repetition of events in the second half of the poem; the other is the ending of the *Odyssey*. Odysseus comes to his own house in Book Seventeen, and he is in it, disguised, until the end of Book Twenty-One. In that time he is twice insulted by the disloyal maidservant Melantho and twice by the goat-herd Melanthius, and three times things are thrown at him by different Suitors. That has often made scholars suspect that these apparently duplicated scenes come from different poems, roughly cobbled together to make up our *Odyssey*. But if we follow this series of scenes we see Odysseus asserting himself more and more, as his true nature shines out of his ragged disguise.

Thus when the Suitor Eurymachus insults him, saying that he would himself be glad to give him a job of work, but doubtless he is too idle, Odysseus replies with a magisterial rebuke, proclaiming himself a good ploughman, good reaper, and good warrior – 'Let us compete, and you will see!'

You are violent and your mind is ungentle, and no doubt you think you are a great man and a brave one, because you mix with few and second-rate people. But if Odysseus were to appear, the doorway would be too narrow for you as you fled.   (18.381–6)

The Suitors, in this series of scenes, grow feebler and feebler, the superiority of Odysseus and Telemachus becomes more and more menacing; and we see that it really is a sequence, not a random agglomeration. There remains a question, perhaps, whether so long a development is entirely compatible with suspense; but that is another matter. The poet has lingered lovingly over it.

The end of the *Odyssey* is an ancient problem. When Penelope has finally been convinced that this man is indeed Odysseus, she asks him of his future, and she is told of the journey he must make among people who know nothing of the sea, and of their eventual happiness together. Then her maid prepares their bedroom and lights their way to it: 'they then entered with joy upon the old ritual of their bed' (23.296). We are informed by learned notes originating in antiquity that the great Alexandrian scholars including Aristarchus (see section 7) 'made this the end of the *Odyssey*'. That is a cryptic remark: in what sense did they regard it as the end? Aristarchus went on, apparently, deleting passages as spurious in what follows (23.310–43, 24.1–204), and it is hard to see how he could have done that had he simply regarded it as spurious in its entirety. On the other hand, the poem cannot possibly end with the line quoted, excellent as it is both as a verse and (in English) as a conclusion; because in the Greek it is introduced with a particle, *men*, which belongs in a clause or sentence which will be answered by another. It would be like ending an English work with a

sentence starting 'They on the one hand' — and no other
hand. It may be that our derivative ancient notes come from
and misrepresent a statement to the effect that 'the action of
the *Odyssey* is complete at this point'.

What follows is in fact odd in some ways. It begins with a
very long passage in indirect speech, an unHomeric device
(23.310–43). It goes on with a second scene in the Underworld, shorter and less impressive than Book Eleven, and
featuring unheard-of things — the White Rock, the Nation of
Dreams, ghosts who can enter Hades before the funeral of
their bodies (contrast Elpenor, 11.51–4, and the soul of
Patroclus, *Iliad* 23.71ff). Odysseus calls on his old father and
cannot resist using on him another of his untrue tales, before
finally identifying himself when the poor old man swoons
with grief. The scene has often been found heartless. Yet the
parallel with the *Iliad*, in which two whole books follow the
killing of Hector and re-establish harmony, first between
Achilles and the other Greeks, and then between Achilles and
his enemy's father Priam, suggests that the truce-making and
hatchet-burying of Book Twenty-Four really is part of the
Odyssey. It ties up the ends, indeed, in a less profound and
moving way than the last book of the *Iliad*, a supreme point
in Homeric poetry; but it does give a reasonably satisfactory
conclusion to the events of the poem.

16. Men and gods

All serious poetry of early Greece involves the gods. As we
saw in section 11, the presence of the divine agents, visibly at
work in what happens, enables the poet to show the meaning
of events and the nature of the world. In the *Iliad* we find a
rich cast of gods and goddesses. Some take the side of the
Achaeans, others that of Troy. There are lively disputes over
the nectar on Olympus, as the divine partisans support and
oppose their chosen mortals. Sometimes they go down — all
save Zeus — and intervene personally on earth, on the bat-
tlefield or in private interviews. From moment to moment
they seem unedifying: 'Homer makes his men gods and his

gods men' comments a great critic in late antiquity, and he was thinking primarily of the *Iliad*. Gods even suffer, and the shady pair Ares and Aphrodite, who are on the Trojan side and whom the poet seems not to like, are actually wounded by mortal warriors, while even Zeus grieves for the death of his son Sarpedon. Yet the suffering of gods is soon over and lacks the tragedy of that of men, and the phrase 'sublime frivolity' fits them well. For they can be, at moments, sublime as well as frivolous.

The *Odyssey*, too, has some scenes of the assembly of gods, and Athena comes down constantly to intervene among men. But the divine cast-list is considerably less extensive, with a number of the great gods of the *Iliad* barely appearing, such as Hera, Apollo, Artemis, and Hephaestus, and no more lively scenes of divine dissension. Poseidon does not want Odysseus to get home, and so the subject is simply not raised among the gods until a day comes when he is away (Book One); and when Odysseus says to Athena that he was not aware of any help from her on his perilous journey, she replies that she did not want to fight with Poseidon her uncle (13.316–19, 339–43). That was not the way of the gods of the *Iliad*.

Fewer gods, then, appear, and they do not behave in the old turbulent manner. The frivolity of the gods, indeed, is now concentrated in the story which Demodocus sings to the pleasure-loving Phaeacians: a frankly saucy tale, this time, again with Ares and Aphrodite in an undignified role. As in the *Iliad*, these two are rather the poet's butts. And even that spicy tale is a variation on the central theme of the *Odyssey*, a wife's chastity menaced in the absence of her husband. On earth that ends in tragedy, whether she yields like the guilty wife of Agamemnon or resists like the virtuous Penelope; in heaven there is temporary embarrassment, laughter, and the adulterous pair go off to their separate cult centres and resume their existence of splendour:

Springing up, Ares went to Thrace, while she, the laughter-loving Aphrodite, went to Cyprus, to Paphos, where she has a piece of land and an aromatic altar. There the Graces bathed her, and anointed her with immortal oil, like that which perfumes the deathless gods, and dressed her in lovely garments, a marvel to behold. (8.361–6)

But the gods draw the same moral from this story as men draw from the destruction of the Suitors: 'Ill deeds come to no good' (8.329). Odysseus, when he kills the Suitors, spares the herald Medon with the words 'Fear not, Telemachus has saved your life, so that you may know in your heart, and tell other people, how good deeds are far better than evil-doing' (22.372–4).

Olympus is becoming, if not exactly respectable – we still hear a good deal of the irregular offspring of gods, a story-pattern which originally catered to the aristocratic pride of noble families – at least morally defensive and anxious to be justified. The first words we hear from Zeus in the poem are on this very theme. Meditating on Aegisthus, he breaks out

Alas, how men blame the gods. They say that evils come from us, while it is they by their own reckless folly who incur suffering beyond their fate: even as Aegisthus now won the wife of Agamemnon, beyond his fate, and killed him when he came home. He knew it was sheer disaster, for we had told him so in advance, sending Hermes the keen-eyed Argus-slayer, not to kill the man nor to court his wife, for vengeance would come at the hands of Orestes . . . so spoke Hermes, but his good advice did not convince the mind of Aegisthus: now he has paid for it all at once. (1.32–43)

The Zeus of the *Iliad* kept good and evil in jars in his house, and at his pleasure gave to some a mixture, to others evil unmixed (*Iliad* 24.527–33); this sort of careful self-justification was by no means in his style. We are reminded (cf. section 14) of the care taken in the *Odyssey* to exculpate Odysseus from responsibility for the loss of his men. The Suitors, too, like Aegisthus, and like the crew of Odysseus, are warned before they are destroyed (2.161–9, 20.345–72). Justice, in the *Odyssey*, is both done and seen to be done. Men suffer 'beyond their fate' by going out of their way to incur disasters. 'Fate' is, of course, not to be thought of as a fully developed fatalism; it is more a matter of 'what was coming to them'.

Odysseus is repeatedly addressed as 'Zeus-born', *diogenēs*.

Exactly how he descends from Zeus is not explained. In some sense Zeus is 'father of gods and men' (1.28, etc.), but he is father more particularly of kings and heroes, and in the case of Odysseus the epithet seems no more than a mark of regal and heroic rank. Poseidon is the father of the Cyclops, as he is father in myth of many other monsters felt as akin to the abysses of earth and sea. This particular connection, though, is probably an invention of the poet for the sake of his plot, which wants an angry sea-god.

The gods have supreme power, but they are not omnipotent. Omnipotence is of course not easy to reconcile with polytheism, as gods oppose each other. Men have free will and are responsible for their actions. Athena can indeed put courage into a man's heart (3.76), or an idea: Odysseus would have been broken against the rocks, for instance, had not Athena put it into his mind to cling on to them (5.427). We even hear of a Suitor, the comparatively decent Amphinomus, when he has been warned by Odysseus to get out in time, taking serious thought:

Indeed he foresaw disaster. But even so he did not escape his doom: Athena bound him fast to die at the hands and mighty spear of Telemachus. Back he went and sat down on the chair from which he had risen. (18.151–7)

Such a passage, striking as it is, does not possess the full theological implications which it might have in a Hebrew or Christian work, and painful questions of predestination and free will are not really raised. An important part of the meaning is that Amphinomus is a loser and will in fact be killed. Athena in classical art often carries in her outstretched hand a miniature figure of herself: that is Athena *Nikē*, Athena Victory. Her favour means success, and it is no less true to say that she favours Odysseus because he is a winner, than to say that he wins because of her favour. At times her interventions seem essentially otiose: Odysseus could well have thought of clinging to the rocks by himself, and indeed it is not clear that the poet means much more than that he had a sudden salutary thought. At other times she is a fully imagined person with likes and dislikes. An excellent example is the scene in Book Thirteen where she joins Odysseus on Ithaca. First she appears in disguise, and he tells her one of his usual false tales. The goddess smiles, strokes him with her hand, and assumes a different form: that of a handsome and accomplished woman. She tells him that lies are pointless with her, and that she loves him because, like her, he is intelligent and versatile; and the two of them sit together and plan the death of the Suitors (13.221–374). No male god is ever as close to a mortal as this. Their relationship is not sexual, but it has a special quality which goes with the difference of sex. Athena is more intimate with Telemachus than with anyone other than Odysseus – the connection is an hereditary one – but while she is thoughtful towards Penelope, sending her sweet sleep and comforting dreams (e.g. 4.795ff, 16.603ff), she does not meet her, and their relationship has no intimacy.

The destruction of the Suitors involved the hand of Athena as well as that of Odysseus. That marks him as a great hero and victor, and also enables the people in the poem to say, with truth, that the gods do not permit conduct like theirs. Odysseus himself says 'It was the doom of the gods which slew them, and their own wickedness' (22.413). Penelope at first ascribes the act to 'one of the immortals' indignation at their violence and evil-doing' (23.4). When old Laertes hears the news, his response is to cry 'Father Zeus, after all you gods are still on high Olympus, if indeed the Suitors have paid the price for their criminal violence' (24.351–2). The Olympian gods may not look like the embodiment of pure virtue, but it is important to the *Odyssey* that they do respond to the inextinguishable cry of the human heart for justice.

17. Men and women

The focus of the *Iliad* is narrow and intense. It is a poem of men, and of men at war. Above all what interests the poet is the warrior facing death at the hands of another warrior: the instant transition from the god-like brilliance of life to death, darkness, oblivion. He uses every poetic device to make it important and vivid to his audience. We do indeed meet women, old men, a small child, and they are made convincing, but all are seen in their relationship to the warrior – Hecuba the mother of the hero, Priam the suffering and helpless old father, Briseis the captive concubine, Andromache and her baby, the wife and child for whom it is so hard and yet so necessary for the hero to face death.

The *Odyssey* is very different, a poem of wide interests and sympathies. Animals, servants, exotic foreigners, craftsmen, beggars, women: all are objects of its curiosity. It is no good to be a modest vagrant (17.577); it is better to beg in the town than in the country (17.18); outdoor servants like to talk face to face with the mistress and hear her news, and have a meal, and go off with a present (15.376–8). Such humble but vital truths interest the poet of the *Odyssey*. The dying dog Argus, and the slave-woman who is weaker and slower than the others at grinding corn, and the young sailor Elpenor, 'none too valiant in war and not well settled in his wits', who falls off a roof when drunk and breaks his neck (17.291, 20.105, 10.552): all are seen with dispassionate sympathy.

In the *Iliad* the hero stands against other heroes. In the *Odyssey* the individual stands against the group, Odysseus against his insubordinate sailors, Telemachus and Penelope and Odysseus in turn against the Suitors. When Odysseus is alone among the Phaeacians we see the same pattern, though with less hostility: the isolated individual with no resource but his wits, confronting a self-confident and homogeneous mass. It is not an accident that the Suitors remain so little individualised.

Not only is it now one against many: in this world the hero must contend not only with his equals but also with turbulent inferiors. Odysseus' sailors are mutinous, and they find a ring-leader in Odysseus' kinsman Eurylochus (10.429ff, 12.278ff), apart from their disastrous action, caused by jealousy, of opening the bag of the winds (10.34–55). The Suitors' aim is sometimes to get the kingship for themselves, sometimes apparently to divide it up and abolish it (16.384–6). The dead Achilles worries that his old father Peleus may now, in the absence of his son, be 'dishonoured' by his subjects (11.494–503). Odysseus' false tales sometimes turn on similar questions of status. He may claim to be the illegitimate son of a wealthy man, excluded from inheriting by his legitimate brothers at the old man's death (14.199–215), or even a man who was in bad odour with a great chief because he insisted on leading his own contingent rather than subordinating himself, who was consequently treated unfairly in the division of booty, and who avenged himself by killing the chief's son, ambushing him from behind a wall (13.256–68). These stories of Odysseus are close to real life and the events of the stormy archaic period; there is little high-flown heroism about them. Yet still it is notable that this last one, which shows the narrator resorting to guile against a stronger opponent in a dispute over property, echoes the plot of the *Odyssey* in an unheroic form, as the Song of Demodocus gives the triangle of husband, wife, and lover in a transposed style.

In such a world loyalty is a treasured quality. Some of Odysseus' servants are faithful, and they are rewarded. Others are disloyal. The maidservants are hanged, Melanthius the goatherd comes to a sticky end. The fidelity of Odysseus' wife is crucial to the story, and the contrast between her and the disloyal wife of Agamemnon is repeatedly emphasised. Antinous, most brutal of the Suitors, is violating a special obligation to Odysseus, who defended his father when he was on the run (16.424–33); the vixen Melantho was brought up by Penelope like her own daughter, yet she betrayed her. If the sailors of Odysseus had only listened to his advice, they would have got safely home.

Also important is self-control, not showing one's feelings. As Odysseus declares his identity to Telemachus he weeps – 'while before he had constantly restrained it' (16.191), and his immediate instruction to his son is

If the Suitors insult me in the house, your heart in your breast must endure it as I am ill used. Even if they drag me out by the feet or pelt me, you must look on and control yourself. (16.274–7)

Telemachus must obey: when Antinous throws a stool at his father,

Indignation swelled in the heart of Telemachus as he was struck, but he did not shed a tear but shook his head in silence, plotting vengeance.   (17.489–91)

Still more must Odysseus himself dissemble and endure, even in the climactic moment when Penelope sits beside him in a flood of tears, melting like snow,

while Odysseus felt pity in his heart for his wife's weeping, but his eyes were as unmoved as horn or iron, and by guile he concealed his tears.   (19.209 – 12)

Penelope, too, has long learnt this lesson of distrust and dissembling. The trick of the web was worthy of her husband, and she never loses her self-control with the Suitors.

The habit of distrust bites so deep that Odysseus cannot resist 'testing' his old father with yet another false story rather than revealing himself at once (24.235ff). While Penelope, to whom hungry scroungers are always coming with false tales of her husband (14.122), not only refuses to believe the assurances of the disguised Odysseus about his return and also rejects an emphatically unambiguous dream (19.559ff): she cannot even bring herself to believe in him when he has declared himself and the Suitors lie dead. Still she sits undecided, looking at him, unable to make up her mind. Telemachus is indignant, but Odysseus smiles. He thinks he is in command of the situation, but in the end it is he who is tricked. Penelope refers to their bed as if it had been moved, and Odysseus loses his serenity –

So she spoke, testing her husband, but Odysseus addressed his prudent wife with emotion: 'Wife, that was a speech which grieves me to the heart. Who has moved my bed?'   (23.181–4)

The choice of the marriage bed is an unmistakable symbol of the solidity of their relationship: it cannot, surely, be moved. By knowing the secrets of that bed, and by the emotion which he refused to show when she wept in Book Nineteen, Odysseus at last identifies himself to his wife; by her self-command and guile she shows herself to be like him, the true wife for the hero of the *Odyssey*.

To men, women are inscrutable. In the *Odyssey* that

characteristic is dwelt upon with pleasure. Odysseus never knows why Calypso suddenly let him go; the Suitors are completely baffled by Penelope; Circe, with her sinister magic passing directly into the offer of sexual union (10.316–35), terrifies the sailors and remains opaque to the hero. Nausicaa, who has just had a dream about getting married and been told in it that she should do a big wash, to make sure that there are clean clothes for her men-folk to wear on the day, asks her father for the waggon and the servants but does not mention her real motive: 'for she felt embarrassed to mention lusty marriage to her dear father' (6.66). Penelope disconcerts her son by refusing to fall into the arms of this man who has killed the Suitors, and she outwits Odysseus himself in the end. Sometimes the motif seems to be developed for its own sake, as when Queen Arete, after the great build-up which insisted that *she* was the person to whom Odysseus should go, remains silent when he supplicates her (6.303–12, 7.53–77; 7.142–71), so that an elderly nobleman must tell Alcinous to do something. Her silence is unexplained, until suddenly she breaks it with the tricky question, 'Who are you? Where did you get those clothes?' (7.237).

On his travels Odysseus meets a complete range of female types. There is the loving Calypso who wants to marry him, and the more hard-boiled Circe, who is happy to share her bed with him but who says, when he finds the courage to announce that he wants to leave, 'Don't stay in my house against your will' (10.489). He meets Nausicaa, the ingénue, who had been dreaming of getting married, and who drops him some hints on the subject: if you are seen with me, people will say 'Who is this good-looking man with Nausicaa, a stranger? Where did she find him? He will be her husband next' (6.275–7). Her mother, the formidable queen Arete, is not so favourably impressed by this stranger turning up in garments which she recognises, and all the hero's tact is called for (7.237ff). Then there is always Athena, feminine but asexual, a sort of elder sister. Telemachus even meets Helen and is impressed by her: 'There I saw Argive Helen', he tells his mother (17.118). She represents yet another type, a glamorous lady with a notorious past but fully in command of the situation and of her husband, whom she charmingly upstages at every turn. When Telemachus has first arrived, Helen makes an effective entrance and at once says 'Do you know who these young men are, Menelaus? Surely this is the son of Odysseus, Telemachus.' 'Just what I was thinking!' says the amiable hero (4.138–48). And at Telemachus' departure, when an obvious omen is sent to them, the well-bred Pisistratus says to Menelaus 'Tell us, is that omen meant for us or for you?'

So he spoke, and warlike Menelaus pondered in his heart how best to answer. But Helen of the long dress anticipated him and said 'Listen to me, and I will interpret it, as the gods put it into my mind and as I think it will be.'   (15.160–73)

This gallery of feminine types is developed, much more than the women of the *Iliad*, simply as interesting in themselves. Yet, interesting as they all are, Odysseus in the end wants Penelope. Calypso offers him immortality with her – an immortality outside the real world and its problems and rewards: 'You might stay here with me in this house and be immortal, for all your longing to see your wife, whom you pine for day after day' (5.208–10). Odysseus evades that tricky point with tact, emphasising to Calypso not his wife ('indeed she is inferior in looks to you, for she is only mortal') but 'going home'. But we have seen that their reunion is made into much more than what the logic of the old story demanded, the collecting of a passively waiting wife. She must be really satisfied about him, not just won as a prize; and their meeting is highly emotional.

This is a strongly devoted family, in fact. We hear, of the nurse Eurycleia, that Odysseus' father Laertes paid a very high price for her when she was young, 'And he respected her equally with his wife, and never had to do with her in bed, but avoided his wife's indignation' (1.430–3). Laertes is broken by the absence of his son and the death of his wife: 'Her death grieved him most and plunged him prematurely into old age' (15.357). As for his wife, she died of grief at Odysseus' absence, as her ghost tells him (11.197–203). The poet seems to be echoing what Odysseus himself says: there is nothing better than husband and wife living together in harmony, 'and they themselves know it best' (6.182–5).

18. Society and geography

We saw in section 2 that the *Odyssey* presents, generally speaking, the world of the eighth and seventh centuries B.C., but as a past time and with some degree of deliberate stylisation; bronze instead of iron, for instance. The memory still exists that Agamemnon was a Great King, in some sense above other kings, but this idea, already in the *Iliad* not really understood by Homer, has lost all substance in the *Odyssey*. In reality each little community is entirely independent. Each community is ruled by a king, *basileus*: Nestor is in Pylos what Odysseus is in Ithaca. But the word *basileus* is not unambiguous. Odysseus was king, but when the rude Suitor Antinous says to Telemachus 'May Zeus never make you *basileus* in Ithaca, which is your right by inheritance', Telemachus replies by saying that it is no bad thing to be king, if Zeus grants it: 'But in truth there are many other kings (*basilēes*) among the Achaeans in sea-girt Ithaca: one of them can have it, since Odysseus is dead; but I will be master of my own house and my own servants' (1.385–98). Among the Phaeacians Alcinous is unambiguously declared to be king: after the death of Nausithous, who founded the city, 'Then Alcinous was the ruler, with wisdom from the gods' (6.12). Yet he seems to be little more than first among equals, and says himself 'There are twelve pre-eminent kings (*basilēes*) among the people who have sway as rulers, and I am the thirteenth' (8.390–2).

This is important because the constitutional position in Ithaca is unclear. Sometimes it seems that the Suitors are perfectly the social equals of Telemachus, and any one of them might be king; at other times it is suggested that Telemachus must be dead before this can happen, and consequently they plan to kill him. At times it seems that the kingship will go with the hand of Penelope: Antinous, we are specifically told, was aiming at the kingship (22.50–3), and Telemachus says that another of the Suitors, Eurymachus, plans 'To marry my mother and get the position of Odysseus' (15.521–2). Yet of course this is not how inheritance worked in a strongly patriarchal society like Greece, and at other times it is envisaged that Penelope will leave Ithaca, go back to her father, and be married from his house. Thus Athena says to Telemachus 'As for your mother, if her heart desires remarriage, let her go back to the house of her kingly father: they can make a wedding and provide a dowry for her' (1.275–7), and Telemachus makes that a feature of his speech at the Ithacan assembly: 'Let the Suitors apply to the lady's father, in the proper way!' (2.50–4). And at times the implication is that it is only the house and possessions of Odysseus, not the kingship, that will go to Penelope's husband, or perhaps only the house and not even the possessions (2.335, 16.385).

All this cannot be reduced to a sociologically reliable picture of a society but is fundamentally inconsistent. The reasons for this state of affairs are of several sorts. First there is confusion about the historical circumstances of the Mycenaean period in which the poems are set. In those days there were real kings in the land, so tradition says; but what they were like, or how their kingship worked, is no longer clearly understood. The poet gives his King Alcinous the grandest palace he can invent, but when it comes to power Alcinous behaves like an exponent of collective leadership. The old kingdoms are, it seems, a thing of the past for the singers, who are familiar in real life only with the aristocratic regimes which in the eighth and seventh centuries were struggling with the traditional royal families all over Greece, or had succeeded in dispossessing them. The Suitors on Ithaca in a way represent that same political struggle, several times suggesting among themselves that the kingly possessions should not go to any one man but be divided up among them all: 'Let us keep his livelihood and his property ourselves, dividing it up fairly among us, and let the house go to Penelope and the man who marries her' (16.384–6). As for the question of Penelope's new husband getting the kingdom, that is required by the logic of the story, which demands that Odysseus be on the point of losing everything – wife, possessions, throne. It is the way things work in fairy stories: 'Then he married the king's daughter and became king in his turn', and also in myths like that of Oedipus, who becomes king of Thebes by marrying the king's widow. This is less a matter of historical realities than of the way in which events are determined by the needs of the narrative. Rather than invoking primeval matriarchy, we should think – if we want a 'rational' explanation – that with Odysseus gone and his son either a minor or killed, possession of the king's widow and palace would at least be a strong card for an ambitious man. The difficulty can be seen as arising from the introduction of something like real politics into a story which was originally a myth of a different character.

There is also visible an interest in other types of society. Among the Cyclopes, we read, 'They have no assemblies to reach decisions nor any established laws, but they dwell among the mountain peaks in caves, and each lays down the law to his children and his wives, and they take no account of each other' (9.110–15). That state of primitivism contrasts with the over-civilised Phaeacians, who live for games and pleasure, and among whom the king is hardly distinguished from his nobles, while the queen is extraordinarily influential, like Queen Helen in the luxurious land of Sparta. The poet also has a sharp eye for fertile terrain. The goat island adjacent to Cyclops-island is described as if in a prospectus for a colony (9.105–60), with its woods, goats, pastures, potential plough-land, natural harbour, and water supply. We feel ourselves to be in that eighth- and seventh-century world in which Greeks were lining the Mediterranean with colonies. The Phaeacian settlement is actually described just like one, Nausithous building a city wall, and houses and temples, and dividing up the land (6.8–10): what Odysseus sees when he gets to the Phaeacian town is a typical Greek settlement (6.262–9). This can shade off into the fantastic. In Africa the fertility of sheep is amazing, they lamb three times a year (5.85–9); in Laestrygonia 'the paths of day and night are close together', and man who needed no sleep could earn two salaries, one as an oxherd and one as a shepherd (that is, the nights are so short: 10.82–6). In extreme contrast, the miserable Cimmerians never see the sun at all, but permanent night covers them (11.14–19).

A few things can be said about the society envisaged by the poem. There are two classes, the noble and the non-noble. There are slaves, but their position is not the worst: when Achilles wants to name the most miserable of earthly lots, he says 'I would rather be a hired labourer working for another man, for a landless man with little livelihood, than rule over all the dead' (11.489–91). That, apparently, was the worst of all; and we observe that some slaves in the poem are quite well off. Dolios, who is a slave, has a wife and six sturdy sons (24.497), and Eumaeus, also a slave, has been able to buy a slave of his own, Mesaulios (14.449). Another instance of the difficulty of constructing a society from the data of the poem is that the household of Odysseus contains fifty women servants (22.421), but he hardly seems to have any men. That is dictated by the poetical need that there shall neither be an army of loyal retainers to help him face the Suitors nor a mass of disloyal ones. Therefore they do not exist – until at 23.147, in the mock celebration which serves as a cover, we hear of music and the 'dancing of men and well-dressed women'. They can only be men of the household.

There are a few experts, men with skills who can be called in – prophets, wood-workers, healers, singers (17.384–5) but there is no middle class. All men, even kings, work with their hands: Odysseus boasts of his skill at reaping and ploughing, and he made and inlaid his own bed (18.365–75, 23.189–204). All men are country-men, and the city is only a place of refuge and meeting. There are traders, but they may also do some piracy and some slaving (3.71–4, 15.415–84): heroes, too, live in a way which may include all three activities, but the aristocrat can profess to despise the professional trader, wrapped up in his cargoes and his profits (8.161).

One of the keenest interests of the *Odyssey* is in good manners. The etiquette of host and guest is, as we have seen, a constant theme: it has both an aesthetic and also a moral aspect. One of the reasons for Telemachus' journey to Pylos and Sparta is to show him how to behave in the great world. Initially he is shy, unwilling even to address an older man like Nestor — 'It is embarrassing for a young man to interrogate an elder' (3.24). He acquires polish and self-confidence. Social equals exchange compliments and presents; servants are treated with urbanity. It is only the Suitors who insult servants (21.85) and also overwork them. The poet's wide sympathies, which extend to beggars and dogs, see with indignation the plight of a servant-woman whose job is to grind corn, the most unenviable of tasks; she is the weakest, still toiling away when the others have finished and gone to bed. Odysseus hears her voice as she curses the Suitors who have worn her out with work: 'May this be the last and final time the Suitors enjoy their feast in Odysseus' house: they have exhausted me with painful toil grinding the corn — let this be their last dinner' (20.116–19). The poet is confident that so homely a touch will not be incongruous in a high heroic epic.

What we have seen in the case of society is true also of the poem's geography. Ithaca is presented vividly, a rocky island:

In it is a mountain, Neriton where the leaves quiver, conspicuous; around Ithaca are many islands close together, Doulichion and Same and wooded Zacynthus. Itself it lies low, the last in the sea to westward — the others are more to the east and the rising sun. It is rough, but a fine nurse of men.   (9.21–6)

So says Odysseus of it, adding 'There could be nothing sweeter to me than to see my country.' There are intractable problems about the exact identification of all these places, and argument has raged among scholars ever since classical antiquity. The island still known as Ithaca is not the furthest to the west of the neighbouring islands, and it is hard to find Doulichion and Same without putting them, or one of them, on the mainland. It seems that the poet had less exact knowledge of these places than he succeeds in suggesting. Again we must remember that among the places on his Ithaca is a cave with two entrances, 'One towards the north, to be trodden by men, but that towards the south is for gods: men do not go in that way, but it is a path for the immortals' (13.109–12). That sounds more like a symbolic place than one which you can find on a map. By 'Ithaca' the poet means the island which is still called by that name, but his picture of the local geography is inexact.

The wanderings of Odysseus and Menelaus take them to places much more exotic. Some are real enough: Odysseus has been to Delos, he tells us (6.162), and Menelaus to Egypt (4.351ff). But the poet's knowledge of Egypt is slight indeed – he describes the Pharos island, which is less than a mile from the shore, as lying 'As far from Egypt as a speedy ship can sail in a whole day, with a brisk wind blowing behind her' (4.356), while conversely he imagines Thebes, which is four hundred miles from the sea, as near the coast (4.125–7). When Odysseus leaves Troy he begins by plundering nearby peoples, like the Cicones of Thrace, who were allied to the Trojans in the *Iliad* (*Iliad* 2.846); but then comes a storm, land vanishes from sight, all directions are lost, and for nine days (a typical rather than an exact number, cf. 7.253, 10.28, 12.447, 14.314) the ship is carried helplessly. Then it reaches land: the land of the Lotus-Eaters. The storm has blown Odysseus off the map and into the world of fable, the seas sailed by Sinbad, where there are witches and giants. Thereafter we do indeed find indications of direction and distance – Calypso's island is in the west, as he must sail eastwards from it, with the Great Bear on his left (5.272–7), while Circe's is in the east, 'Where the home of the Dawn is, and the risings of the Sun' (12.3–4) – and ever since antiquity people have tried to trace Odysseus' course, locating the Lotus-Eaters in North Africa, or in Malta, and so on. But that cannot, in principle, be done. The Alexandrian scholar and scientist Eratosthenes (died 194 B.C.), the first man to give an accurate measurement of the circumference of the earth, observed drily that 'You will be able to chart Odysseus' wanderings when you have found the cobbler who made the bag that held the winds.' That is to say, a world which contains things like that is not our mappable world of prose. And it may be worth adding that the adventure with Circe, which is set in the *Odyssey* on an island, has exactly the look of a tale set in the great forests of the north: 'I went up to a high point to see if I could make out signs of cultivation and hear human voices. I climbed up a rocky look-out point, and I thought I saw smoke rising up through the thick trees and bushes' (10.146–50). That is the house of the witch in the wood, the setting of the story of Hansel and Gretel and so many others. It may be much older than any association with sailors and an island.

19. The values of the *Odyssey*

We saw in section 14 that the plot of the *Odyssey* created a tension between two types of heroism: the dashing Iliadic fighter like Achilles, pitted against other heroes in equal battle, and the wily opponent of giants and witches, who must use guile against overwhelming force and impossible odds. Achilles chooses a glorious death at Troy rather than long life without fame, but Odysseus will die in his bed, a very gentle death in sleek old age (11.134–6; 23.281–3). To reach that goal he must show himself a survivor, prepared to beg, to use guile, to accept humiliations, to conceal his feelings. 'I hate that man like the gates of hell who hides one thing in his heart and says another': there speaks Achilles (*Iliad* 9.312–13). 'I am Odysseus son of Laertes, known to all men for my guile': there speaks Odysseus (*Odyssey* 9.19–20), who is warmly complimented by Athena on his unmatched skill in deception and cunning (13.291–9), and whom we hear tell many plausible lies. Over the body of his great enemy Achilles calls on the Greeks to raise the cry of exultation: 'We have won great glory: we have killed the noble Hector' (*Iliad* 22.391). Over the bodies of the Suitors Odysseus represses Eurycleia's cry of exultation: 'Rejoice in your heart and do not cry out: it is not right to exult over the bodies of slain men' (*Odyssey* 22.411).

Odysseus speaks freely and often of the imperious necessities of the belly. He begs the Phaeacians to leave him alone to eat:

Let me dine, full of grief though I am: there is nothing more shameless than the hateful belly, which bids one remember it perforce, even when one is worn with grief and suffering. So it is that I have grief at heart, yet my belly constantly bids me eat and drink, and makes me forget all my sufferings and bids me fill it up.

(7.215–21)

That speech shocked readers in later antiquity ('Not even Sardanapalus would have said such a thing'), and it is only the most extreme of a series of utterances of Odysseus on the subject – compare 15.344, 17.287, 17.473, 18.53. Again Achilles provides a point of comparison. In the Nineteenth Book of the *Iliad* there is a lengthy argument on the subject of eating. Achilles demands that the army be led out to battle at once, unfed, to kill Hector and avenge the death of Patroclus; it is Odysseus, we observe, who puts the opposite view, that men fight better after a meal – 'It is not with the belly that the Achaeans must mourn the dead' (*Iliad* 19.148–225). The fiery heroism of Achilles is impatient of this sort of thing.

It is also too exalted to be passionately interested in possessions. When Agamemnon is finally forced to restore to Achilles the captive girl Briseis, the subject of the great quarrel, he gives with her a massive recompense in treasure. Achilles' response is to say 'As for gifts, you can give them if you like, as is right, or you can keep them yourself: now let us join battle!' (*Iliad* 19.146–9). When King Priam brings treasure to ransom the body of his son Hector, Achilles does not look at it, and he actually wraps the body in some of the garments which Priam brought as part of the ransom (*Iliad* 24.580–1). Odysseus, by contrast, is keenly concerned with possessions. He comes home in the end with 'more treasures, bronze and gold and garments, than was his share of the booty of Troy' (*Odyssey* 5.38–40; 13.135–7). We feel the poet's own pleasure that despite his tribulations he does not come home impoverished. His first care in Ithaca is the careful bestowal of this treasure. He even went so far, among the Phaeacians, as to say

If you were to bid me to stay here a year, promising passage home and giving me gifts, even that would I accept; indeed it would be much more to my advantage to come home to my own country with

my hand full, and I should meet more respect and hospitality from
all those who saw me on my way to Ithaca.   (11.356–61)

What of the lonely Penelope? we ask. But Odysseus is confident that she would understand. He tells her himself, while he
is in disguise, that 'Odysseus would have been here long since,
but it seemed to him more advantageous to collect money by
begging over the world' (19.282–3) — in fact he is unrivalled
at doing it. And the reader is bound to notice the importance
of themes of property in the poem as a whole.

In all these ways, the attitude to property, to food, to telling the truth, Odysseus stands closer to the common attitudes
of men. He is brave and he has fought well in battle, but he
is more at home in night expeditions, ambushes, stratagems.
He finds himself in situations in which Achilles cannot be imagined: you simply cannot be Achilles in the cave of a
Cyclops. The heroism of Achilles represents the highest flight
of the heroic which early Greece could imagine, living for
glory and accepting death. Odysseus is not just less heroic
than that; he also has human attachments of a sort which
Achilles does not. Achilles is unmarried and alone in the
world. His mother is a sea-goddess, his father far away, of his
son he says that he does not know whether he is alive or dead
(*Iliad* 19.327), and as for the girl Briseis, 'I wish she had died
before she caused such a quarrel' (19.59–62).

Odysseus, as we saw in section 17, comes from a close and
affectionate human family, and his attitude to Penelope and
Telemachus is that of the good husband and father. Such a
man does not throw away his life for glory, and the *Odyssey*
gives its own answer to the *Iliad* when it makes the dead
Achilles speak. Odysseus addresses him in flattering terms: no
man has ever been more blessed, he was honoured like a god
by his comrades in life, and now he is mighty among the dead.
Achilles brushes this away: 'Do not console me for death,
bright Odysseus: better the poorest fate on earth than the
highest position among the dead' (11.482–91). We must hear
in this scene the retort of the *Odyssey* to the glamorous and
passionate heroism of the *Iliad*: they would sing a very different tune, the poet suggests, when they really faced the facts

of death. The heroism of the survivor is not such a small thing.

Odysseus is forced to learn the power of self-control, to keep silent and not go in for easy heroism. He fails once, early in his adventures, at the end of the ordeal with the Cyclops. Having kept his nerve and his self-possession, remembered to give a false name instead of his real one, remembered that it will not do to attack the sleeping monster and kill him with his sword (9.299ff) − that would be heroic, but they would all be doomed without the power to roll away the mighty stone − and having kept his men up to the mark in the act of blinding the monster, he yields to a temptation of heroism in revealing his own name in a shout of triumph (9.491−535). That was a disastrous mistake, and we do not see him repeat it. In his own house he endures in silence, accepts insults without immediate response, and bides his time, even watching Penelope weep while appearing unmoved (19.209ff). We see that it is not easy: when he lies in his improvised bed and listens to the laughter of the unfaithful maidservants as they go off for their last night of pleasure with the Suitors, 'As a bitch, standing over her litter, when she does not recognise a man, growls and prepares to fight: so did his heart within him growl at their misdeeds.' He calls his heart to order: 'Endure, my heart: you have endured worse, on the day when the irresistible Cyclops was devouring my trusty men, yet you kept your courage until cunning brought you out of the cave where you expected to die.' His heart obeys, but with difficulty, while the hero tosses and turns like a blood-pudding seething over a fire (20.1−23). The striking passage, with its memorable similes, emphasises the demanding moment.

The power to conceal one's feelings is important in a world full of treachery and hostility. But for those who, in such a world, show themselves worthy to be trusted, the response is warmly emotional. Eurycleia calls Odysseus her child, touchingly so in her first utterance on recognising him: 'In truth you are Odysseus, dear child: and I did not know you for my lord before I had touched you' (19.474−5). Both

'dear child' and 'my lord': the juxtaposition is effective. The
devoted servant feels both feudal loyalty and personal love.
When Telemachus comes back from Sparta he goes straight
to Eumaeus' hut:

He came to meet his master, and kissed his head and both eyes and
both hands: a big tear fell from him. As when a father embraces his
son in love, a beloved only son, who is returning from a foreign land
after ten years. . .   (16.14–21)

That is a remarkable simile. In the presence of the unrecognised father, who has been away for twenty years,
Eumaeus embraces his young master with parental love; the
moment is one to dwell upon.

   Odysseus' self-revelation to Eumaeus and Philoetius leads
to a tearful embrace, with kisses on both sides and tears on
theirs − but not on his (21.221–6): his eyes were as dry as
horn or iron even when his wife wept, sitting beside him
(19.211–12), and he does not allow himself to weep until the
Suitors are dead and the loyal maidservants surround him −

They flocked round and greeted Odysseus, and embraced and kissed
his head and shoulders, seizing his hands. He was overcome by the
sweetness of the desire to weep and wail, and he recognised them all.
                                                           (22.498–501)

At last the ice can melt, as it does again in the meeting and
embrace between husband and wife in the next book. Fidelity
is rewarded, and the guard finally can be lowered. Still there
lie perils ahead, but the ultimate outcome will be happy, with
gods benevolent and love restored in the family and prosperity among their people. Penelope can now accept this without
complaint, saying 'If indeed the gods will grant us a better old
age, then I have hopes that we shall escape from our sufferings' (23.265–87). From the narration of suffering we are to
draw serenity: the gods devise disasters, Odysseus is told, that
there may be song among men (8.579), and to listen to that
sad song gives delight. Listen and learn, Penelope was told:
the gods bring unhappiness on many others besides you
(1.353–5). In the end Odysseus and Penelope have learned

that hard lesson. Life is full of unhappiness, but that is what is transmuted into song. They achieve harmony with that process and learn, as we are to learn, the lesson of the *Odyssey*.

Chapter 3

The *Odyssey* and after

20. The after-life of the *Odyssey*

The two Homeric poems were decisive for the whole course of Greek literature. No less important than the fact that two such masterpieces stood at the very beginning of that literature was the fact that they never went out of fashion or ceased to be enjoyed. That is very unusual: poems like the *Song of Roland*, the *Nibelungenlied*, or *Beowulf*, usually become old fashioned, cease to be heard or read, and are rediscovered, if they are lucky, by later scholars. In Greece the effect of *Iliad* and *Odyssey* was unbroken.

The greatest of the descendants of the epic was Athenian tragedy. Plato called Homer 'the first and greatest of tragic poets', and the people of the epic reappear as the heroes and heroines of the Athenian drama. Odysseus is a character in the *Ajax* and *Philoctetes* of Sophocles (a good character in the former, a bad one in the latter), and in the *Hecuba* of Euripides; he is much spoken of in Euripides' *Trojan Women* and *Iphigeneia in Aulis*. Generally speaking tragedy gives him a bad press, presenting him as unscrupulous and deceitful. The conscious seeking after the high style also owed much to Homer; no less important is the fact that Homeric epic contains so much dialogue, often lively and passionate, the very stuff of tragedy.

The *History* of Herodotus continues many of the interests of the *Odyssey*, especially the vivid dialogues, the prominence of women, and the great accounts of travel and of foreign countries, their political constitutions and social customs. The narrower focus of Thucydides on war, with the exclusion of ethnography and of women, can be seen as a return to the concerns of the *Iliad* from those of the *Odyssey*. Our poem is also the ultimate ancestor of the ancient novels, which are stories of parted lovers, wanderings, and reunions, and so of the novels of modern Europe. Such picaresque novels as *Gil Blas* and *Tom Jones* show the influence of the wanderings and amours and happy ending of the *Odyssey*.

Epic poems continued to be written in antiquity. They were the work of literary men who used the pen, not of illiterate singers; but the artificial dialect of Homer, his metre, and some colouring of Homeric formulae and vocabulary, remained obligatory for epic poets. The *Argonautica* of Apollonius of Rhodes, written about 260 B.C., is a competent surviving example. The Argonauts sail like Odysseus and undergo various adventures before their successful return. The love motif, never quite romantic in the *Odyssey*, now becomes more important, and the passions of Medea are among Apollonius' chief interests and most successful effects. When the heroes meet Circe or pass through the Clashing Rocks, for instance, the influence of the *Odyssey* is very clear.

Roman literature actually began, in the view of later Romans, with a translation of the *Odyssey* into Latin, made by a Greek slave named Livius Andronicus, about 220 B.C. Like all Latin works, it called the hero by an Italianised form of his name: Ulysses. Any native productions earlier than Andronicus were simply doomed to perish, once Rome was introduced to the high style and formal elegance of Greek literature. As with other peoples who came into contact with Greece, indigenous works began to seem, both in literature and the visual arts, unbearably crude and provincial. Andronicus began the arduous labour of creating in Latin – an undeveloped language of an unsophisticated people – a literary style capable of rendering the great Greek works and of engendering others which could stand comparison with them. That was the crucial moment for the literature of Rome. The struggle lasted nearly two hundred years: finally Virgil was master of such a style, and in it he created the central masterpiece of Latin literature, the *Aeneid*.

The *Aeneid* is a great epic, in hexameters, about the heroic age, with the personal conflicts and interventions of gods. It even is planned by Virgil in twelve books, a gesture of modesty towards the Homeric epics in twenty-four. Aeneas, a Trojan survivor, makes his way through the Mediterranean to Italy, where he will found the city which is the ancestor of Rome. The poem aims to combine both *Odyssey* and *Iliad*: wanderings in the first half, including a descent to the Underworld, and battles in the second. Aeneas follows Odysseus in narrating his earlier adventures after dinner (he saw the Cyclops in the distance and rescued one of Odysseus' men, accidentally left behind). Virgil extends this Odyssean motif by making Queen Dido fall in love with Aeneas as he tells his moving tale. That means that when he leaves her, as Odysseus leaves Calypso, the result this time will be tragic. The theme also lent itself to development in opera, from Purcell's *Dido and Aeneas* to *Les Troyens* of Berlioz; more directly Odyssean is Monteverdi's *Ritorno d'Ulisse in Patria*, on the hero's homecoming. Helen's sojourn in Egypt (*Odyssey*, Book Four) suggested the plot of Euripides' tragi-comedy *Helen* and of Richard Strauss' witty opera *Die ägyptische Helena*.

Through the *Aeneid* the epic style of Homer became the accepted style of high Latin verse, and so passed into the literatures of Europe. Similes, set speeches, the active and personal role of the gods: these things were the regular furniture of epic and the elevated forms of verse. Pope indeed says of the Homeric gods, 'Whatever cause there might be to blame them in a philosophical or religious view, they are so perfect in the poetic, that mankind has ever been since contented to follow them . . . after all the various changes of times and religions, his gods continue to this day the gods of poetry.' The whole conception of Milton's *Paradise Lost*, with war in heaven described in Homeric battle scenes, and with heroic characters making grand speeches, depends on the Homeric and Virgilian modes. Alastair Fowler points out that the relationship is not simply one of verbal and narrative echoes: 'Milton's allusions to earlier epic are so consistent as to constitute a distinct strand of meaning in the poem.' Only one echo can be mentioned here, the opening line of *Paradise Lost*:

Of man's first disobedience . . .

The *Odyssey* opens with the word 'Man', as the Muse is asked to tell the singer of the man Odysseus. Virgil opened his *Aeneid* with a phrase intended to recall both the *Odyssey* and the *Iliad*, which opened with 'Wrath':

> Arma virumque cano
> (Arms and the man I sing)

Milton begins with *man*, recalling *Odyssey* and *Aeneid*, as the subject of the Muse's utterance ('Sing heavenly Muse', line 6), and immediately turns to strife and death (the *Iliad*) but he goes on

> With loss of Eden, till one greater man
> Restore us, and regain the blissful seat,
> Sing heavenly Muse . . .

His poem will be like a classical epic yet also different: not one man, a hero, but two men, and one of them is more than a man, Christ who is God incarnate. Such effects are made possible by the perceptive use of the classical tradition.

Homer was 'moralised' in antiquity. The Roman poet Horace tells a friend that Homer is a better teacher of ethics and morality than any professor of philosophy, or indeed than formal religion. It was the lust and folly of Paris which started the Trojan War, and it was the angry passions of Achilles and Agamemnon which caused the disasters of the *Iliad*. Odysseus, on the other hand, is a handy example of the power of virtue and reason, resisting the temptations of Circe's cup and the Sirens' song, and by self-denial and mastery over the passions finishing in happiness (*Epistle* 1.2). The sententious *Télémaque* of Fénelon (1699), an enormously successful work telling the story of Telemachus with profuse moralising, was thus, although heavily Christian, in an ancient tradition.

Virgil makes his Aeneas go down to the Underworld and see the unhappy and the happy dead. That was to have far-reaching consequences, among them the *Divine Comedy* of Dante. Virgil's book of the dead is very clearly in the tradition of the *Odyssey*, and Dante's great poem explicitly follows Virgil, not only in many details but also in the whole conception of a journey through the next world, from the punishment of sinners to the fields of the blessed. In the *Inferno* he includes Odysseus himself, tormented in an undying flame ✓ because he would not acquiesce in the God-set limits of the world but insisted on sailing through the Pillars of Hercules (the Straits of Gibraltar) and was wrecked for his presumption on the Mountain of Purgatory. The passage, in Canto 26, is a splendid and moving one:

'O brothers!' I said, 'who through a hundred thousand dangers have reached the West, short time of waking remains to your senses; do not deny to it the experience of the world behind the sun, the world unpeopled. Consider your lineage. You were not made to live like brutes, but to follow excellence and knowledge.'

And so they sail on and are lost. By contrast, Joachim du Bellay gave memorable expression to his own yearning to return home from exile in a sonnet which opens 'Happy is he who, like Ulysses, has made a good voyage' − 'Heureux qui comme Ulysse a fait un bon voyage.'

That invention by Dante is different from the Odysseus of Homer, who plans to age and die in peace at home, when he can get free of his tribulations. It echoed in the ears of Tennyson, whose poem *Ulysses* is a noble statement of the yearning for adventure and experience before death.

> Come, my friends,
> 'Tis not too late to seek a newer world.
> Push off, and sitting well in order smite
> The sounding furrows; for my purpose holds
> To sail beyond the sunset, and the baths
> Of all the western stars, until I die.
> It may be that the gulfs will wash us down:
> It may be we shall touch the Happy Isles,
> And see the great Achilles, whom we knew . . .

The Lotus-Eaters, another of Tennyson's finest poems, is also based on the events of the *Odyssey*.

The dissatisfied and wandering Odysseus re-appears in the extraordinary *Odyssey* of Nicos Kazantzakis (1938). In this enormous allegorical work Odysseus resumes his travels, abducts Helen, takes part in the destruction of the decadent civilisations of Sparta and Crete, finds the source of the Nile, founds a utopian city, becomes a yogi, sails on an iceberg, converses with Death. In English the most important twentieth-century contribution is Joyce's *Ulysses* (1922). Set in Dublin, this vast work, uniquely brilliant in virtuoso stylistic display, presents events of ordinary modern life on a framework of the *Odyssey*. The land of the Lotus-Eaters is represented by a visit to a Turkish bath, the episode of Circe is enormously expanded into a bizarre scene in a brothel. Leopold Bloom, the Ulysses-figure, is bourgeois, not heroic, but by the end of the book he shows that by prudence and endurance he can survive and overcome the risks and humiliations of life.

The great Spanish poet Calderón in the seventeenth century wrote two plays about Odysseus and Circe, one voluptuous, the second pious and penitent: *Love, the Supreme Enchantment*, and *Sorceries of Sin*. Goethe planned, and commenced, a romantic tragedy about Odysseus and Nausicaa, in which the young girl was to fall in love with the stranger and kill herself in despair. Shakespeare makes Ulysses a character, sage and disenchanted, in his bitter play *Troilus and Cressida*. Rubens was among the artists who painted Calypso; Turner's magical painting of Odysseus and Polyphemus is to be seen in the National Gallery in London. Even set in the future we find films like *2001: a Space Odyssey*. It would be hard to think of another work than the *Odyssey* which has given such varied evidence, over so long a period, of an inexhaustible fertility, both in literary form and also in fundamental plot and story.

Guide to further reading

Items marked with an asterisk (*) can be read with profit by those who do not know Greek.

(a) Editions, commentaries, translations

There is a good text of the poem in the Oxford Classical Texts series, ed. T. W. Allen; two volumes.

The one volume edition by P. Von der Mühll (Basel, 1945 reprinted 1986), gives a useful brief running summary (in Latin) of the editor's views, in the nineteenth-century analyst tradition, of the order of composition of the elements of the poem.

*There is an edition in the Loeb Classical Library with facing translation, archaic in style, by A. T. Murray (1919).

The unpretentious commentary by W. B. Stanford (London, second edn, 1959, 2 volumes) is generally helpful. A more extensive and up-to-date commentary, published with text and facing Italian translation, is in process of appearing in six volumes, edited by A. Heubeck, S. West, J. B. Hainsworth, and others (Mondadori, 1982–). This is now appearing in English (Oxford University Press, 3 volumes), the most reliable commentary available. R. J. Cunliffe, *A Lexicon of the Homeric Dialect* (London, 1924) is a helpful book.

*Of the translations mentioned in section 9, that by Robert Fitzgerald appeared in 1961 (New York), that by *Richmond Lattimore in 1967 (Chicago), that by *Walter Shewring in 1980 (Oxford). *Pope's translation, often reprinted, is available with full apparatus in vols. 9 and 10 of the Twickenham Edition of the *Complete Poems of Alexander Pope*, ed. M. Mack (New Haven and London, 1964). *Pope's own introduction to his version of the *Iliad* is of interest to any reader of Homer.

Two rewarding works on translation are: *Matthew Arnold, *On Translating Homer* (1861); and *H. A. Mason, *To Homer through Pope* (London, 1972), mostly concerned with the *Iliad*, but taking a broad view of the subject. Also *the Epilogue on translation in Walter Shewring's version of the *Odyssey*.

(b) Background

*A. J. B. Wace and F. H. Stubbings (eds.), *A Companion to Homer*

(London, 1962), full and reliable on most background matters. *M. I. Finley, *The World of Odysseus* (2nd edn, Harmondsworth, 1979) discusses the sociology described or assumed by the *Odyssey*. *O. Murray, *Early Greece* (London, 1980) and *J. Boardman, *The Greeks Overseas* (2nd edn, London, 1980) are helpful on the historical setting. *T. B. L. Webster, *From Mycenae to Homer* (London, 1958) is interesting on the Oriental connections. *W. Burkert, *Greek Religion* (Oxford, 1985) is an excellent general account of the religion of early Greece, including Homer.

On oral poetry: the papers of Milman Parry are collected as *The Making of Homeric Verse*, ed. Adam Parry (Oxford, 1971). *The long Introduction by Adam Parry is interesting on Milman Parry and gives a critical account of the oral theory. *A. B. Lord, *The Singer of Tales* (Harvard, 1960) deals with Homer and the Yugoslav tradition. G. S. Kirk (ed.), *Language and Background of Homer* (Cambridge, 1964), is a collection of important papers; also G. S. Kirk, *Homer and the Oral Tradition* (Cambridge, 1976). Norman Austin, *Archery at the Dark of the Moon* (Berkeley, 1975): the long first chapter makes important criticisms of the oral theory. *An important general work, with implications for Homer, is Ruth Finnegan, *Oral Poetry* (Cambridge, 1977). G. Germain, *La Genèse de l'Odysée: le fantastique et le sacré* (Paris, 1954) collects comparative material and advances bold theories about the original function of the stories in the poem. D. L. Page, *Folktales in Homer's Odyssey* (Harvard, 1973) is an approachable work on the subject.

(c) Literary interpretation

*There is an interesting collection of critical essays: *Twentieth-Century Interpretations of the Odyssey*, ed. Howard W. Clarke (Englewood Cliffs. N.J., 1985). *Also by Howard W. Clarke, *The Art of the Odyssey* (Englewood Cliffs, N.J., 1967). *The large book by G. S. Kirk, *The Songs of Homer* (Cambridge, 1962) discusses literary aspects of the Homeric poems as well as technical ones. *Hermann Fränkel, *Poetry and Philosophy in Early Greece* (Oxford, 1975) opens with a thoughtful and stimulating discussion of the Homeric poems. D. L. Page, *The Homeric Odyssey* (Oxford, 1955) is a brilliantly written (sometimes over-written) treatment of the difficulties in the poem, which in Page's view rule out unity of authorship. Bernard Fenik, *Studies in the Odyssey* (Wiesbaden, 1974) is a careful and subtle attempt to explain the difficulties and defend the coherence of the poem. *Jasper Griffin, *Homer on Life and Death* (Oxford, 1980), gives a general interpretation of the Homeric epics. See also *Paolo Vivante, *The Homeric Imagination: A Study of Homer's Poetic Perception of Reality* (Bloomington, 1970). *The first chapter of Erich Auerbach, *Mimesis* (Princeton,

1953), 'The Scar of Odysseus', is a brilliant if exaggerated essay on Homeric style. On the similes: C. Moulton, *Similes in the Homeric Poems* (Göttingen, 1977). *W. J. Woodhouse, *The Composition of Homer's Odyssey* (Oxford, 1930) is gentlemanly in manner (no references to other modern works) but makes interesting points. *The theory that the poem was composed by a woman: Samuel Butler, *The Authoress of the Odyssey* (London, 2nd edn, 1922).

Four German contributions: F. Klingner, 'Über die vier ersten Bücher der Odyssee', reprinted in his *Studien zur griechischen und römischen Literatur* (Zürich, 1964). K. Reinhardt, 'Die Abenteuer der Odyssee' reprinted in his *Tradition und Geist* (Göttingen, 1960) (collected essays). W. Schadewaldt, *Von Homers Welt und Werk* (Stuttgart, 4th edn, 1965). H. Strasburger, 'Der soziologische Aspekt der homerischen Epen', reprinted in his *Studien zur alten Geschichte* (Hildesheim, 1982).

(d) After-life

*W. B. Stanford, *The Ulysses Theme: A Study in the Adaptability of a Traditional Hero* (Oxford, 2nd edn, 1963). *Brooks Otis, *Virgil: A Study in Civilized Poetry* (Oxford, 1963), and *C. M. Bowra, *From Virgil to Milton* (London, 1945), on oral and literary ('secondary') epic. *J. L. Myres (ed.), Dorothea Gray, *Homer and his Critics* (London, 1958), on the history of attitudes to the poems.